IN THE KINGDOM
OF THE
Thunder Dragon

Joanna Lumley

IN THE KINGDOM
OF THE
Thunder Dragon

BBC BOOKS

*To my mother, Beatrice,
who was too young to go with them*

My warmest thanks go to the camera crew; Graham Smith, camera:
Tony Meering, sound: Chris Vile, assistant cameraman and stills:
Hugh Thomson, director: Laura and Harry Marshall of Icon Films, our producers:
Mark Harrison, Major John Davie and John Drury for all their work and support;
Susan Proctor, Charlotte Lochhead and Linda Blakemore for making the book look
so good, and Dr Michael Aris for showering his endless wisdom on the project.
Finally, I would humbly like to thank Her Majesty the Queen Mother whose
kindness and hospitality enfolded us during our time in Bhutan.

This book is published to accompany the television programme
Joanna Lumley in the Kingdom of the Thunder Dragon
first broadcast in 1997 and produced by Icon Films Limited
All colour photographs © Chris Vile except for p12 © Eric Lawrie,
p72 © Tom Owen Edmunds and p74 © Joanna Lumley
All black and white photographs are from the Weir archive

First published 1997
© Joanna Lumley 1997
The moral right of the author has been asserted in accordance
with the Copyright Designs and Patents Act 1996

ISBN 0 563 38329 1

Published by BBC Books, an imprint of BBC Worldwide Limited,
80 Wood Lane, London W12 0TT

Set in Simoncini Garamond and Stone Serif by BBC Books,
Printed in Great Britain by Cambus Litho Limited, East Kilbride
Bound in Great Britain by Hunter & Foulis Limited, Edinburgh
Colour separations by Radstock Reproductions Limited, Midsomer Norton
Jacket printed by Lawrence Allen Limited, Weston-super-Mare

Contents

Introduction

There were twenty-four tins in all; large, round battered containers, each about the size of a tricycle wheel, with faded labels in my grandmother's handwriting – Lhasa, Tibet, Sikkim and Bhutan. Inside the tins were reels of film, some 35mm, some 16mm, some negative, others positive. They were in a very fragile state: sprockets were damaged, they had become highly flammable and when a strand of film was pulled loose it often stopped with a sickening crack as though it were made of sticky tape. The ancient suitcases which housed them had only been able to give them mediocre protection as they were shunted from go down to store-house for sixty years, in extremes of temperature; from Kashmir and Bombay, to Kenya and Kent. Several canisters were missing, lost long ago from a coracle which capsized crossing a river in Tibet, emptying all its contents into the rushing grey torrent which swept them under and away. All the footage had been shot by my grandmother Thyra (pronounced 'Toora') Weir and her eldest daughter, my aunt Joan Mary. They used the state-of-the-art cameras of the 1930s, wind-up contraptions which they operated without tripods. None of the younger members of the family had ever seen the films: by the time we were old enough to be interested in our grandparents' extraordinary travels, the spools of celluloid had declined into a condition of such brittle fragility that to manoeuvre them on to a projector would have been to risk damaging them beyond repair. It was extremely frustrating: the more we could find out about Bhutan in the 1990s, the more we longed to see moving evidence of what it had been like sixty-five years before. True, we had black and white photographs (those that had survived the capsized coracle) which were taken by my grandfather; and we had diaries kept by Granny and Joan Mary, and we tracked down my grandfather's detailed report to the Government of India. We also had the beautiful religious silk hangings they'd been given, gold and silver boxes, wonderful woven cloth, and we had Joan Mary's vivid memories and drawings... but what we didn't have was watchable film.

Until the Moviola, that is. Quite suddenly, on a hot afternoon in Soho in 1993, and seemingly without effort, the ancient, bronze-coloured crackling ribbons of film poured their secrets out on to videotape. The images were immediately unforgettable: flickering black and white, even partly damaged as they were, nothing could detract from the majestic splendour of the landscapes and the pomp and ceremony of a great state occasion in one of the remotest countries in the world.

Joan Mary's daughter, my only girl cousin, persuaded me with the greatest ease and speed that life would be intolerable if we didn't make plans to visit Bhutan as soon as possible. Using the old diaries, maps, photographs and film, we would retrace our grandparents' journey as far as we could and see how things had changed. We would make a film of our travels (I use the word 'we' pretty loosely; in this case it means a very small crew from an independent film company; with my cousin Maybe and me, we numbered seven). There was no time to lose: Bhutan admits only 2500 visitors a year and has fairly stringent attitudes to some programme-makers, so we had to apply at once. We would have the chance to renew the friendliest relationships forged between the Bhutanese Royal Family and our grandparents, and we would try to identify the exact locations described in the diaries.

*Left: My grandmother, Thyra
and her eldest daughter Joan Mary
in riding kit in the garden in Sikkim.
The dogs went with them. Their
wonderful diaries, films and sketches
inspired our recreation of the journey
sixty-five years later.
Above: Joan Mary, Maybe (left)
and me on board a troopship in
Hong Kong, 1949.*

In the biographies of Buddhist saints we read how journeys were sometimes undertaken for their own sake: anything good or bad encountered
along the way can be turned to the purpose of achieving enlightenment.
Whatever was to happen to us as we travelled across the tiny Buddhist
kingdom would be appropriate and acceptable: the journey was to be as
important as its goal.

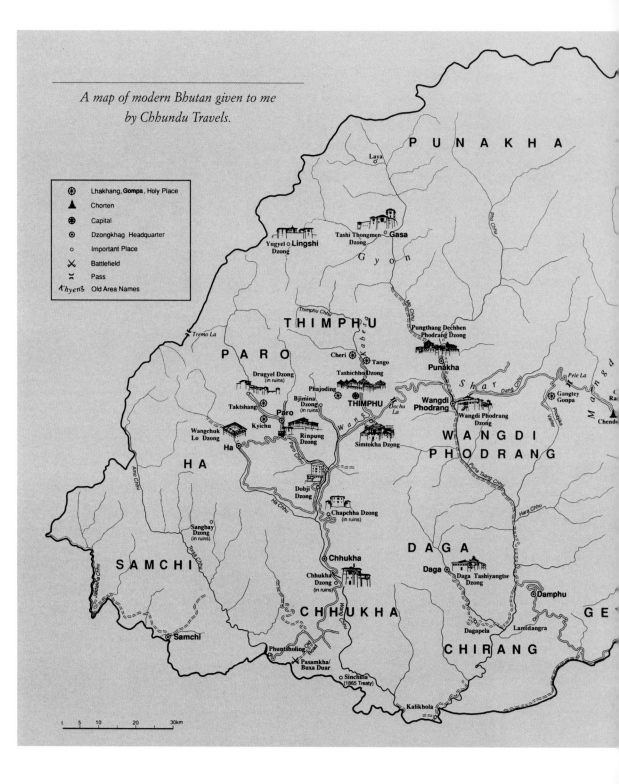

A map of modern Bhutan given to me by Chhundu Travels.

Legend:
- ✪ Lhakhang, **Gompa**, Holy Place
- ▲ Chorten
- ✪ Capital
- ⊙ Dzongkhag Headquarter
- ○ Important Place
- ✕ Battlefield
- ≍ Pass
- *Khyeng* Old Area Names

PUNAKHA

Laya

Yugyel Dzong   Lingshi   Tashi Thongmen Dzong   **Gasa**

Gyon

THIMPHU

Thimphu Chhu

Pungthang Dechhen Phodrang Dzong

→ Tremo La

PARO

Cheri   ✪ Tango

Drugyel Dzong (in ruins)   Tashichho Dzong   **Punakha**

Phajoding

Bjimina Dzong (in ruins)   **THIMPHU**

Shar Dang Chhu   Pele La

Gangtey Gonpa

Taktshang   Paro   Dochu La

Wangdi Phodrang   Ra

Chende

Wangchuk Lo Dzong   Kyichu   Rinpung Dzong   Simtokha Dzong   Wangdi Phodrang Dzong

Ha

WANGDI PHODRANG

HA

Dobji Dzong

Chapcha Dzong (in ruins)

Sangbay Dzong (in ruins)

DAGA

Daga   Daga Tashiyangtse Dzong

SAMCHI   Chhukha

CHHUKHA   Chhukha Dzong (in ruins)

Damphu

Dagapela   Lamidangra

Samchi

GE

CHIRANG

Phuntsholing

✕ Pasamkha/ Buxa Duar

Sinchula (1865 Treaty)

Kalikhola

0 5 10 20 30km

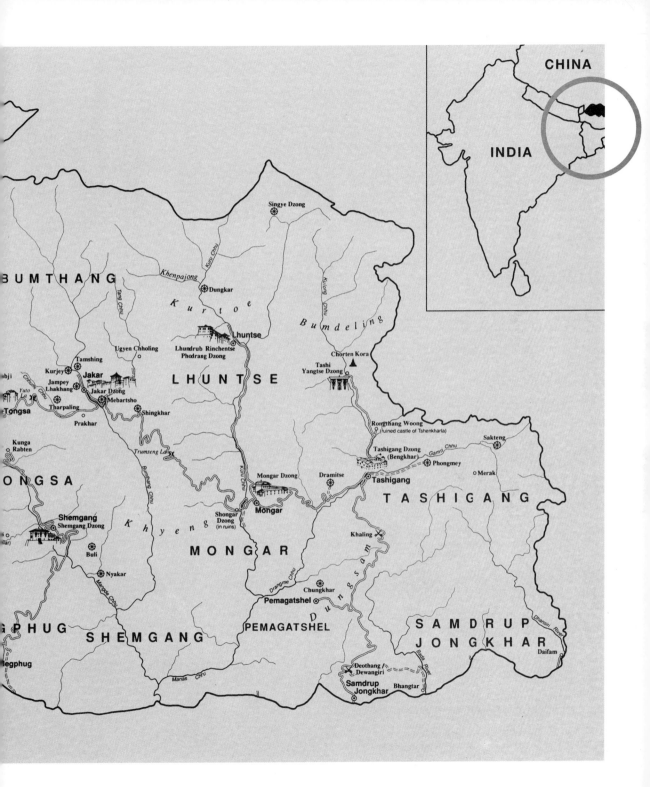

Chapter One

How it Began

The Himalayas lie like an immense snowy necklace around the throat of Tibet. At the northwest end of the range they crash into the mighty Karakorams (and it was there that I was born); then they sweep down over the top of India, through Nepal (where the Gurkhas come from, and with whom my father was a regular officer); and then they roar towards China in the northeast. Hanging from the necklace is a pendant of great beauty and that is Bhutan. To the north of the kingdom the snowy peaks of Chomolhari and Gangkar Punsum remind you that you are among the big boys, no fooling, mountains of over 24,000 ft. Then the country begins to lose height, until at her southern borders with India she has a lush, sub-tropical climate with mangoes, bamboos and oranges. To the east her neighbour is the Indian state of Arunachal Pradesh, which is still almost a blank on the map; and to the west lies Sikkim, once, like Bhutan, an independent kingdom, but now part of India.

*The kingdom of the Thunder Dragon, Bhutan. The valleys magnify
both sound and silence, so that a bird-call may be heard easily from two miles
away and rivers far below sound as though they're flowing directly underfoot.
The skies seem extra-immense.*

My grandfather, Colonel Leslie Weir (1883–1950)
looking splendid in the uniform of the Fifth Cavalry. In family
photographs he appears in many guises, looking equally
at home in full Tibetan regalia or an old tweed coat.

My maternal grandfather, Colonel Leslie Weir CIE, was the Political Officer resident in Sikkim from 1928 to 1932. A Political Officer was a mixture of many things – administrator, ambassador and adviser, in this case to the three regions he was assigned to: Sikkim, Tibet and Bhutan. He was a brilliant linguist and spoke eight or nine languages, conversing in Tibetan with the thirteenth Dalai Lama on that country's external affairs, and running the British Trade Agency in Gyantse under Sir Charles Bell in 1909. He had served in Persia, Baluchistan and Kashmir, married my half-Danish grandmother in Rangoon and was, in my father's words, 'a bloody nice chap, one of the gentlest men I ever knew'.

The Residency in Sikkim was in Gangtok, and it was there in June 1930 that my grandfather received 'a cordial invitation from His Highness the King of Bhutan to visit him at Bumthang, the capital of his State'. It was decided that the insignia of the KCIE, Knight Commander of the Most Excellent Order of the Indian Empire, which had been conferred on His Highness on the occasion of King George V's birthday, should be presented during the visit. This would be an exciting journey: Bhutan remained shrouded in mystery, its doors and borders closed to almost all foreigners, a country veiled in secrecy known only to itself. My grandmother Thyra would go with him, together with her young sister Dagmar and their eldest daughter Joan Mary: but my mother, Beatrice, was still at boarding school in far-off England, aged only ten and too young to travel with them.

It would be a gruelling trip physically, through Himalayan foothills in January, with no roads or hotels, just pack ponies, stout boots and camping equipment. Grandpa wrote to his mother in Scotland just before they set off: 'Don't worry about Joan Mary. She has had a great time in Delhi and Calcutta but she has not fallen to the lures of rouge and lipstick, nor does she smoke or drink cocktails. She will be leading the simple life with us in Bhutan for the next two months, and then coming home, so I do not think she will succumb to too many temptations.' Joan Mary was then seventeen:

Maybe and I are already fifty, and have long ago fallen for the lures of lipstick, cocktails and cigarettes. We will trek only part of the journey as now there are new tarmac roads and Jeeps and cars; and we will be under canvas only some of the time, as there are now hotels and guest houses. Even so, we will be hard put to match the stamina of our grandparents' expedition, and butterflies of apprehension flit about as we pack up our equipment in London.

The Weirs' journey started in Sikkim, then on through Tibet, on Bhutan's western borders, and over the pass into the Ha Valley. From there it was a three-day march to Paro, where their first official reception was held – the first of many such receptions, but none more splendid than in Paro, where they were met by dancers 6 miles from the town who danced before them all the way. Three miles further on they were greeted by a guard of honour, '... twenty men richly clad in silks, with swords, iron helmets and rhinoceros-hide shields'. Mules and ponies had been sent for their use, tea, fruit and rice were offered, and the *Penlop*, the local governor, entertained them at the monastery, where *lamas* (monks) danced for them in the frosty afternoon.

Our trip, of course, began rather differently. Air India to Delhi, then Druk-Air, the Royal Bhutan airline, via Nepal to Paro. Separated by only sixty-five years, we would join the Weir expedition in the Paro Valley.

Their Highnesses the King and Queen of Bhutan in 1935, four years after Grandpa had presented the King with the KCIE; the regalia can be seen clearly on His Highness's chest. The length of his robe (below his knee) denotes the highest standing in the land. The Queen's superbly-woven robe or kira would be handed down from generation to generation.

Chapter Two

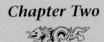

A Pendant
of Great Beauty

Only twelve pilots have ever qualified to land at Paro, the toughest airstrip to negotiate in the world. From Kathmandu the aeroplane flies due east from Nepal, through the spectacular snowy summits of the Himalayas, past (and at a lower altitude than) Everest, past Kanchenjunga and mountain ranges reaching as far as the eye can see, over deep slashed ravines and colossal glaciers. Druk-Air's fleet consists of two immaculate aeroplanes: ours is piloted by Captain George Deserres, an ex-Vietnam veteran with a huge handlebar moustache, who talks his passengers through the dashing approach into western Bhutan. As we descend in a series of steeply banked turns, with wingtips almost scraping the hills, we can see rice fields, long shadows and huge sunflowers. The airport is tiny with a wooden picket fence. Arrivals and departures are in one and the same room; passengers carry their own luggage. The valley is wide and lush with steep surrounding hills dotted with carved wooden houses, their slate or timber roofs weighted down by stones. It is at the same time very like, and completely different from, Switzerland.

The Paro Valley – below the Dzong on the right is the old bridge.

Before we set off on the first leg of our journey we spend a night in the Druk Hotel, about 1000 ft up along a newly made road. The Druk Hotel has wooden balconies and a large stone courtyard with a bonfire in the middle. The night air is creamy and warm. The newest of new moons hangs in the sky, and beneath me, in the darkening garden three floors below, a small ginger dog settles down, wagging his tail at me, to sleep the night. In the starlight the paddy fields stretch away, dotted with poplar trees and willows; and the Paro River glints as it ripples over its stony bed like a Scottish stream. Images of Scotland and Switzerland... but all you have to do is look to the north and there stands the huge, white-walled *dzong*, shimmering in the dusk, terracotta stripes under a golden roof, the first of the fortress monasteries that we see with our own eyes. Hard to tell how tall it is: it must be eight or nine storeys high, but the windows only start at the fifth floor. The walls slope slightly inwards, so it's wider at the base than where the lime-washed walls meet the gorgeously carved underbeams of the roof. Spiritual and secular, dzongs are ambiguous places, symbols of ultimate power uniting peace and oppression. In the past, the common man would shudder as he passed in the shadow of the great fortress-monastery, knowing that the resident warlord had the power over life and death. The light is going and I can't see properly now: the dzong will look after the valley tonight and Maybe and I shall go down to the fire, where some Bhutanese girls are dancing in a graceful circle, small stepping movements and twisting hands and wrists. They are wearing long, wrap-around tunics in fantastic colours with silk blouses and heavy jewellery. Their short black hair shines in the firelight and they grin at us with great friendliness.

*The bridge at Paro. From photographs it doesn't look as though it has changed
at all since the Weir expedition clattered over on horseback, the hoofbeats echoing
above the shallow rapid river. Prayer flags bless those who come and go,
and there are prayer wheels at each end. You could dream here for hours.*

Chapter Three

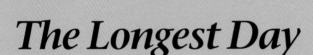

The Longest Day

At dawn the valley is covered with low cloud, quickly burning off under the autumn sun. We pack and leave the hotel and walk down the hill to the Paro river. Children are on their way to school, chattering and clutching their homework, boys in the knee-length tunics and long socks, and the girls, even the tiny ones, in long skirts. Traditional dress is worn everywhere in Bhutan. The men's robe is called the *gho*, the women's the *kira*; the first is like a sort of dressing-gown hitched up around the waist with long sleeves and deep cuffs, while the kira is a length of cloth cleverly wrapped and pinned and worn with a blouse and jacket. Clothes apart, it is like the beginning of a school day anywhere in the world: the dawdlers, the small group, someone with his head in a book, jokes, shoving, running, senior boys looking cool, a small girl eating an apple – 'Hallo!' they say to us, 'Goodbye!' and smile and wave.

Although I settle down to draw the Paro Dzong, a small curious audience distracts me. This little person comes closer and closer and I make some lightening sketches of her enchanting face – all the children we meet are friendly and unafraid. Girls all have their hair bobbed short. Even the tiny ones manage the long skirts of their kiras with graceful ease.

Top: The Weir party on the Ha pass from Tibet into Bhutan. Grandpa on the left is accompanied by Dagmar, Granny and Lieutenant Revel Sinclair. Joan Mary, only seventeen at the time, took the picture. It must have been bitterly cold in January and after the descent into the Ha Valley it was a three-day journey to Paro.
Above: The musicians and the guard of honour waiting to receive and escort them down into Paro. The costumes and uniforms were superb and despite the ice and snow most of the men went barefoot.

In the 1930s there were a few schools, but only for boys; girls were given no formal education. As part of the reception committee for the Weir expedition, '… schoolboys came out to meet us and accompany us for half a mile, each carrying a gay flag. After lunch we inspected them in their school. A proper wrestling enclosure had been made and they all wrestled in pairs and were very good, each having his second, and a chair and wraps and the towel and the usual massage at half time. A crowd came to watch, much interested. The boys are a fine-looking lot and read English and Hindustani very creditably'.

We've started learning a few words of Bhutanese: '*Kuzu zangpo la* – good health' says my cousin Maybe, greeting an old woman, who immediately answers '*Kuzu zangpo la'*, twice, a rather satisfactory exchange.

Maybe is a nickname. Her real name is Myfanwy, but when her mother was expecting her, a fourth child after three boys, everyone said, 'Maybe this one will be a girl'. It was and the name stuck. Surrounded by schoolchildren we walk through a peaceful willow grove, followed by wandering wag-tailed dogs, where the sun slants through woodsmoke on to neat gardens of dahlias and zinnias. There in front of us is an unmistakable landmark from the archive film: the fantastic Paro Bridge, covered over with a dark wood roof, prayer wheels at either end which each traveller spins by reaching into a hand-smoothed socket. Granny wrote, 'We left our camp in state, on our mules gorgeously caparisoned with saddles and cloths of multi-coloured appliqué flannel. Still mounted we crossed the bridge, ascended many steps, crossed the drawbridge surrounded by crowds of people and, led by the dancers and the bodyguard, entered the truly medieval castle'.

Maybe and I look at each other, take a deep breath and start off after them. Our companions on the bridge are two young men, a cow, a schoolboy rushing past late and three grand old women. Above us is the Paro Dzong, which is closed now to visitors so we won't be able to see its fabulous court-yards and temples. Puffing and blowing a bit, we reach the high terrace where a solitary figure waits to greet us. It is the Venerable Mynyak Tulku Rinpoche, the Incarnate Lama, who has heard of our proposed journey and wants to meet us. He points across the valley to the far hills.

'That is the route they would have taken from the Ha Valley to Paro.'

'It was mid-winter, Rinpoche. What would the going have been like?'

'Tough,' he says, his eyes twinkling. 'Very hard frosts and, higher up, heavy snowfalls. By the way, do you know Keanu Reeves? He filmed part of *The Little Buddha* here,' and he spreads his hands out towards the colossal dzong below us, its massive shape shadowing the smooth stone paths and poplar trees turning to gold. Below, the roofs of the Queen Mother's Palace glint among orchards: rice harvesting has just begun and ravens swoop and caw round the old drawbridge. Chillies are hanging out to dry at the windows of houses. They festoon verandas and are spread out on rooftops, red as blood and hot as hell. Woodpiles are neatly stacked against the walls; a cow

---

The Venerable Mynyak Tulku Rinpoche telling us of the route that the Weir expedition took all those years ago in midwinter. Even the short walk up to the dzong has made us slightly out of breath in the hot afternoon. Ahead of us lies the whole journey; we cannot imagine how gruelling the first real uphill climb will be. The grassy area we are standing on is where a soccer match was played after lunch on 25 January 1931, which, Granny wrote '… amused the Paro Penlop very much. Leslie played, so did Lieutenant Sinclair'.

and her calf graze nearby, her bell clonging quietly as she moves. We take our hats off and the Lama holds our hands and blesses our journey. As we set off up the terrifically steep path, we turn to wave. He is watching us, his hands tucked into his sleeves, his dark red robe backlit against the pale valley. He waves and turns back to the monastery. Our trip has begun.

Or rather it has nearly begun. We reach the appointed place where we are to join up with our luggage and all the porters and pack animals but there is not a pony in sight. We settle down on springy grass under the pine trees and eat apples, cold potatoes and hard-boiled eggs. All around us are violets, primulas, Michaelmas daisies, thistles and blue berries. It is so exciting to be in Bhutan and beginning the trek that the three-hour delay is only a tiny cloud on our broad blue horizon.

The pack ponies, when they do arrive, are already tired from a long trek which finished the day before they were sent off to Paro; and in any case, there are only fifteen of them instead of thirty. Our two riding ponies are nowhere in sight. Packing and leaving takes an extra hour and as we trudge off, a light rain begins to fall and soon the rough track has become a small stream. Up and up we go, pausing very often to catch our breath and still our

---

When the pack ponies want to rest they simply stop and puff till they catch their breath. They are all in beautiful condition: their strength amazes us as they stomp uncomplainingly for miles every day. The pony men carefully balance each animal's load, and only entrust the camera to the most sure-footed beast. Being part of a long caravan is a thrilling ancient feeling, as though we are bringing silk and spice from Peking to Palmyra as in the old days of the great Phoenician traders. Slowly and steadily, our trek begins.

Left: Joan Mary's lovely portrait of thirty-four-year-old Raja Topgay Dorji, chief adviser to the King. His title was Deb Zimpön, *which means literally Chamberlain to the Regent. He inherited this title from his father: his son was to become Prime Minister.*

Right: Our adviser, fixer and translator, Namgay. He makes our journey possible, arranging things in advance for our greater comfort. He negotiates with the ponymen's contractor and we depend on him absolutely during the trek. Besides being a demon at liar dice, he collects the music of Muddy Waters. When he's not leading tours, he farms in southern Bhutan.

thumping hearts. The ponies pass us, bells clanging round their necks, little strong slim legs plodding uncomplainingly under the weight of all our gear and the camera equipment. They will be with us for only the first part of our journey. Namgay walks with us like an anxious shepherd. It is important that we don't get too tired or fall too far behind.

Namgay, or Tshering Namgyal, is our guide, translator and fixer – what in the old days might have been called a *dragoman*. He's rather tall, with a natural authority, flawless English and a terrific sense of humour. He collected us off the plane and his will be the last hand we shake when we leave. The most challenging trek in the world is considered to be the 'Snowman', a devilish itinerary which snakes across northern Bhutan for twenty-seven days. Namgay has led that trek seventeen times and is bored with it now. Such a companion is valuable beyond price and we call him Lochinvar, our dashing Highland knight.

My grandfather's rather more senior version of Lochinvar was called Raja Topgay Dorji, 'Tubby' to his English friends. He was chief adviser and right-hand man to the King of Bhutan in 1931, and was ready to greet the Weir party on its arrival. Grandpa wrote, 'At our first camp we found evidence of the unfailing thoughtfulness for our comfort which we experienced from all the officials of Bhutan throughout the tour. Large campfires were blazing in, and around, our fenced camp and temporary huts had been provided for our servants, coolies and ponies'. Raja Topgay Dorji became indispensable to my grandparents, and a trusted friend. In Grandpa's report to the Government of India, paragraph 23 reads: 'My visit to Bhutan entailed much hard work on the part of Raja Topgay Dorji. He accompanied us throughout our tour, and the brunt of the arrangements fell on his shoulders'.

Our blue tents, dusted with frost. No matter how many clothes we wear, we always wake up in the dead of night, shivering. In 1931 when the forebears made their trip it was mid-winter: although they had log fires in each little bamboo hut it must have been wickedly cold, particularly when the north winds blew. In the mid-distance is the dining tent where we eat in the evenings. Breakfasts are always out of doors – very bracing.

One of Namgay's first arrangements for us is to call back two of the pack ponies so that we may ride uphill for the last few miles. Through the trees we glimpse snow-dusted peaks and far below us the darkening Paro Valley. The ponies are saddled thus: one in a pink eiderdown, and one with blue plastic sheet. It's night now and rain is drumming down. Our feet slip, our lungs are bursting and eventually we must clamber on to the oddly-attired backs of the ponies and stamp on upwards. Suddenly another flickering torch appears in the blackness – it is a porter sent to get more ponies from Paro. His torch is a cloth-wrapped stick dipped in oil and lighted – absolutely ancient and efficient. He flies down on feet barely touching the ground. 'Yo!' he cries, and our lot say 'Yo!', and our huge shadows flicker on the forest floor. In pitch black with our torches gleaming like a medieval procession of pilgrims we plod on, all puffing.

At last we reach the camp site, already set up by the advance party: small blue tents, a roaring fire, an excellent dinner and a glass of whisky. We are deathly tired but immensely cheerful. I sleep in my blue thermal underwear. It is very cold inside the tent and it's hard to settle. In my torchlight I can see through the tent flap thick freezing mist and I can hear the ponies munching at the grass by my guy ropes. I can't see where we are, which makes it even more unreal. There are no pillows, so I roll up my soft fleece jacket and breeches in an African cloth I've brought and jam them under my neck. By torchlight, I can see on the map that we should be just underneath Jili Dzong, now ruined and reputedly haunted. Granny's diary says: '... on the top of the pass is the most picturesque small fort', so it can't be that frightening.

Chapter Four

Lake Water Lapping

We are under a blazing, clear blue dawn sky, on a high alpine pasture with views of distant peaks. Ahead of me the ground falls away steeply into thick bushes; behind, perfect against a cobalt backdrop, is the Jili Dzong. Now I can see the pine forests streaming up from the valley and over the pass where last night's rain turned the ground to fudge, and the frost this morning whitens every leaf and blade of grass. The ponies are being rounded up by one of the porter's sons. He has pegged out a long piece of string, staked into the ground at each end. Each pony he catches he hobbles to the line with a little bit of rope tied loosely round its fetlock. There are mules as well – in fact, somehow the other fifteen pack animals have joined us silently in the night and now we have the full quota of thirty. Some graze on as they're tethered, others doze or nip each other lethargically. They are immune to my

The views from every ridge are eye-stretching. Many of the forests appear to be as old as time and Bhutan plans to keep at least two-thirds of them intact. Overleaf: My little pony. The pleasure of being with animals all day makes even the toughest uphill hike a joy. The huge unorthodox bridle shows the bit swinging clearly, well out of the pony's mouth.

sweet-talking: only occasionally does a furry ear turn back to listen. Loading up is very skilled work and each pony man knows his animals, what they can carry and how carefully they walk. The set-up is this: a contractor is approached by the tour guide, and he in turn gets in touch with his pony men, all freelance, who have several animals each. All the beasts like their own team best and get very anxious when separated from their companions. They follow their leader all day and stick together all night when they are set free to graze on the hills. Getting going, packing, filming, eating breakfast takes forever and it's half past nine before we climb the 300 ft up to the Jili Dzong.

The flap and snap of the tall prayer flags greet us as we walk up under the handsome shabby walls. We are on a long ridge with the prayer flagpoles marching away in an irregular pattern. The flags are beautiful – about 18 inches wide and up to 16 ft long. They are stapled or tied to lofty poles topped with a sprig of spruce, or more often a dagger to demonstrate the power of religion. The flags are called *lung-ta*, (wind horses), and you can buy them in shops. They come in red, yellow, blue, green and white, signifying fire, earth, water, wind and purity.

'... Actually, I don't think I've got that quite right,' says Namgay staring up at one. 'They are all for luck, for good fortune and they must be on a high point, if possible in sight of a river so the prayers can be carried down and along and up and away.' Each flag is printed over and over again with Buddhist prayers in beautiful script surrounded by a lion, a tiger, a dragon, a gryphon and in the centre a horse, with what looks like a flaming jewel on its saddle. The flags have all faded, to a torn creamy grey, but the wind hasn't pulled them from their moorings (nor have the ghosts of the Jili Dzong).

It doesn't feel at all spooky up here in the bright morning sun, surrounded by ponies and the friendly porters, cooks and muleteers. Renovation work has started on the dzong, but though we peer through the cracks in the great timber doors into a weedy cobbled yard and rattle at the locks we can't get in.

'What kind of ghosts, Namgay?'

'Oh, just foolish things, spirits and things like that,' he answers airily.

We are standing on glittering boulders of pyrites, the whole ground is twinkling. I collect a few pieces of sparkling... what?... mica? and put them deep into my trouser pocket from where they emerge a month later in London, mirror-bright and unbroken, after an hour in the washing machine on the hot cycle.

I persist with the ghost theme, reading from Granny's diary:

'"The country near the top of the pass is rumoured to be inhabited by the bad spook men of the hills. Tiger and leopard frequent these parts and people are very nervous except in broad daylight."' But Namgay has moved off to herd in a wandering mule and doesn't hear me.

Overleaf: You can get an idea of the height of prayer flags by comparing the size of Maybe and me as we stride past them. At the top there is most commonly fixed a dagger to show the power of prayer. The tall thin flags are stapled or nailed to the poles; the constant winds and weathering eventually drain the colours to a uniform soft grey. The sound they make is extraordinary; a kind of thudding snapping roar. It's not surprising that they're called lung-ta, wind horses. Prayer flags are positioned everywhere – in auspicious and holy places in great numbers, in wayside chortens or behind houses in ones and twos. They are one of the most potent symbols of the Buddhist faith.

We can see our journey spreading out before us through the most beautiful heavily wooded hills and dark valleys. As in all mountains, the weather can change in moments, and by lunchtime the electric blue sky is overcast and we eat our picnic in a light hailstorm, sitting on edelweiss and gentians under spreading oak and beech trees. The advance party moves on to set up camp several miles further on and inevitably one of the camera-carrying ponies trots off after a tent-carrying friend, only to be caught and returned with the greatest difficulty. They whinny and hee-haw to each other plaintively, the sound sobbing out over the rocky ravines.

Granny and Joan Mary were accomplished artists, and whenever they had the opportunity, they sat and sketched. I would love to have been with them and drawn beside them, the wind scattering our pages and freezing our fingers. I remember watching Joan Mary sketching in her enormous chaotic flat in London, where masses of odd and brilliant people eddied and flowed. There were her four children and their friends, living there, drifting away, returning: overseas visitors passing through town, and young ones like me who started their London life under Joan Mary's wing. When she liked the look of someone she would seize a pencil or biro and start drawing. One young man appeared in her sketches again and again. 'A Greek god,' she would murmur, scribbling and gazing, 'absolute heaven.' Granny was passionate about colours, particularly vivid yellow ochre and purple, rust, black and white. No wonder she adored the sights Bhutan had to offer, its temples, dzongs and *chortens*.

Chortens are wayside shrines, some tiny and modest, little more than cairns, others as large as small temples. You must always go clockwise round a holy place, always to the left, and I've noticed that whenever we are close to a dzong with lamas in residence Namgay puts his white, raw silk shawl over one shoulder like a kind of toga. Women put a narrow, shawl-like belt over their left shoulder; a deference, like covering up in a mosque or wearing a headscarf in church. Buddhism permeates Bhutan in the easiest, most natural way: 'The voice of prayer is never silent, nor dies the strain of praise away'. No matter how remote the path, there is always a *mani* (prayer) wall, or prayer flags, or great prayer wheels either housed in little open-sided pagodas or set over rushing streams where the water spins them endlessly, releasing blessings on everything the water touches: the fish who swim in it, the fields watered by it, the humans and animals who drink it.

A black dog has joined us, tail wagging madly and keeping close to the ponies' heels. We suck lemon drops and puff our way up through weird lichen-laced trees, all dead-looking and bare, like a forest in a Grimm's fairy tale. Soon we're in sunshine and evening again, with thunder and rainbows. Suddenly we see our blue tents through the hillside trees and we stomp through a bog to the camp and its plume of smoke. Mindu the cook has prepared an excellent and enormous supper: tomato soup, vegetable curry and rice, followed by fruit salad. We've brought along some gin and whisky which we drink from mugs, and play liar dice in the communal tent. Hot-water bottles are handed out, and when I go to my tent to push it into my sleeping bag I find the black dog inside smiling apologetically. Namgay won't allow him to stay, so I feed him some damp Nice biscuits and he settles on a grassy tuft outside where he sleeps all night, nose tucked into tail, unmoving. In the morning, he will be frosted over like a little toy yak, his thick coat keeping him alive in the bitter frost. There is blazing starlight above and icy diamonds glitter on tents, ponies and grass.

Breakfasts are enormous. Steam billows from Mindu's cooking tent, where he has some Calor gas stoves and low bonfires. Porridge, eggy toast, fried eggs, meat rissoles, chilli sauce, tea, coffee, toast come out to a table set in the open air. While we eat, we write notes and think how to repack our kit more satisfactorily for the day's march. Being with animals all day is very calming: as the ponies are being whistled in to be loaded, another dog appears, a black-and-tan puppy. Both he and the black dog belong to the sons of porters, whose names we are gradually learning: Rinzin, always at the front, Gem Tshering, who has devoted himself to Maybe's welfare and who wears the heliotrope knitted hat she brought out from the King's Road – Sangay, Poba, Nado... I write all their names and all Bhutanese words phonetically, as does everyone past and present. Bhutan itself was once spelt 'Bootan' by earlier travellers, and even Namgay's name can be spelt two ways. The religious silk hangings Maybe and I have known since we were children are written *'thangka'* or *'tangka'* but are pronounced 'tunka'. This liberated spelling is rather a relief but also an anxiety. It would be dreadful to offend by spelling a name wrongly, as if one didn't care. All the flowers and trees will have to be written in English as I don't know their Latin names and the porters scratch their heads and look sorrowful when I ask for the Bhutanese word for sycamore. *Dzongkha* is the official language, but each valley and region has its own distinct dialect, unintelligible to outsiders, and often even to neighbours.

In the cooking tent, Mindu's great breakfast is almost ready.
Coming from the sophisticated kitchens of the west, it is salutary to see
how a superb cook with some knives, old pots, a sieve and an open fire
can make a feast that would be starred by Michelin.

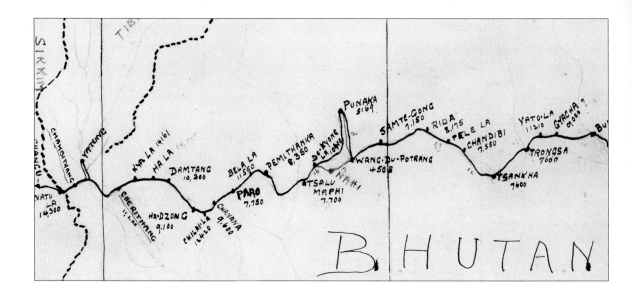

The first half of my grandfather's original chart of the journey.
Thimphu, the capital, isn't shown as it didn't exist then: it would have
appeared to the right of Paro. Note the spelling of Wangdi-Phodrang.

We have Grandpa's map with us and at our picnic lunch we try to marry the names he wrote on his hand-drawn chart (official maps were very sketchy in those days) with those on our newer map provided by Chhundu Travels. Sometimes – often – we have to camp in different places, so the delight of finding ourselves on exactly the same pass is wonderful. Our first lakeside camp will be Jano Tsho, and from the old diaries it seems that it may be a long way but not too taxing. This on my part is pitiful optimism. As soon as we leave camp in the morning we start a long, steep descent through more fantastical lichen-draped forests. We walk down most of the way except when we have to ride for the filming. Our hearts sink during the descent, as down now means up later. We lunch beside a rocky, rushing river in the petrified wood: the menu is rice pilau and green oranges, mango juice, black tea with sugar.

There is a sinister tree trunk straddling the river which we have to cross. My vertigo makes me cling to Namgay's coat, but Maybe is unmoved by the terror and walks over with ease and balance, Gem Tshering helpfully clutching the back of her jacket. The path ahead of us levels out for the length of a football pitch then rears upwards into a breathtakingly steep ascent. We've read about stone staircases and this seems to be one, like climbing again and again to the top of the Eiffel Tower. For good measure, heavy white hailstones start bombing down on us all and the heavily loaded ponies have to rest every ten steps. The porters are gasping for air but roaring with laughter too, high colour in their merry faces, the packs on their backs not seeming to give them grief. My respect for them is immense and I feel like a spoilt, unfit, hopeless bag of lard. Also, the modest way Granny wrote in her diary fills me with humility: '... a steep ascent... a tiring climb... a difficult approach...' and all in deep snow and bitter cold. Here we are, in the milder autumn days with thermal underwear and light warm clothes, and yet we are overcome with fatigue and occasionally despair at the gigantic effort of it all. We are definitely weedier than our splendid forebears, who never complained or commented on discomfort. Pride in their stoicism washes over me and inspires me onwards, resolving not to whine about leg muscles again. We plod on, up and up, and finally there is a little level path (with a thousand foot drop to the right) which leads through rhododendrons to the calm beauty of an oval lake in a natural semicircle of Scottish-looking hills. We're at 13,500 ft and so tired that after supper everyone turns in early, to rootle their tents into sleeping order and rest their stiffening limbs. The cold makes you gasp. The Seven Sisters have just appeared over the horizon and the lake is as still as black glass.

Chapter Five

Dancing in the Moonlight

Altitude has a strange effect on people; at these relatively modest heights, some of our gang have got sickening headaches, and we all trip and stumble over words. Another thousand feet up and even the porters will be getting light nosebleeds. Perhaps it's because I was born in the Himalayas in Kashmir that I feel very well at these altitudes and, although out of training, I feel full of energy and optimism. Those suffering adverse effects didn't have time to acclimatise, but even if they had, susceptible individuals would have got mountain sickness anyway, no matter how carefully they tried to avoid it.

Maybe, despite feeling rather low, has a crack at fly fishing with Namgay at the far side of the lake. The morning is perfect now – hot enough to roll up one's sleeves and so still that you can hear a raven 3 miles away. Some of the pony men have slept in caves in the hillside to be nearer their animals, with only a thinnish bedroll and a small fire to keep them warm. Hill people are the toughest in the world.

---

*On our trek we saw not one house or cottage, not one road or chimney.
Once we met two boys with a bad-tempered yak but the emptiness of this
fabulous landscape cannot be exaggerated. There is ample time for talking
and looking at views, as we travel across the backbone of the world.*

The water from the small tributary streams tastes like icicles, as clean and sweet as snow. Being above the tree line, the mountainsides and gorges are thick with azaleas and dwarf rhododendrons. They are so plentiful that our huge campfires are made entirely from their branches and yet you could never tell we had touched them. This used to be the main road from Paro to Punakha and Wangdi-Phodrang; from time to time we find ourselves walking on paving stones, and occasionally steps are cut neatly into the rock when the path is especially tricky. Some of the ponies and mules walk carefully: others are clumsier. My little steed, called Tshering, walks well; Maybe's pony, Wangdi, steps recklessly on any loose boulder and often stumbles going down steep bits. '*Juh!*' means go forward, gee up, and '*Loh!*' means take care. Mostly I ride without stirrups as the saddlery is unorthodox to say the least, with different lengths of green nylon string tied to the top of the girth, which offer the irons at jockey-length or under the animal's belly. The pony men had kindly thought of our comfort and arranged for Maybe and me to have Western saddles, but once these are positioned over layers of underfelt and small carpets, with another carpet on top, it is rather like being in a howdah on top of an elephant: and to make it more complicated the bridles they've given us are far too big for our little ponies and the bits

Fed by mountain springs and glaciers, the lake water is as clean and clear as glass. It is believed that the British brought young trout to stock the waters for fishing, although how the porters would have managed to carry the little fish in their slopping containers up such immensely steep hills makes you silent with amazement. Our camp can be seen pitched on the far shore. Although the air feels cool, the sun burns your skin quickly at these altitudes.

dangle loosely under their chins. Despite leg aids (flapping and slapping) and vainly trying to steer with the reins, we can't really go where we want and have to content ourselves with following meekly in line. The pack animals wear beautiful smooth, wooden handmade saddles which I covet very much. I'd love to have one, but I think they are the tools of the trade and have been in each pony man's family for years. The pack animals wear no headgear but the leaders of each team have brightly decorated headstalls and wear clanging bells around their necks.

With all our porters, camp attendants, pony men, boys and dogs, we make a pretty impressive sight as our procession leaves the camp, winding up at midday over the azalea-shrouded pass towards the second lake. Grandpa and Granny had about eighty pack animals, including many yak, which would have been provided for their expedition by each district. They carried a prodigious amount: apart from food and clothing, they took enough china, glass and cutlery to entertain the Royal Family, and, of course, an enormous number of gifts from the Government of India to the King to celebrate the great occasion. These included rifles and ammunition, a silver teaset, silver candelabra, clocks, tweed and velvet, felt hats for men, and a toilet set consisting of bowl, ewer, soap dishes and po in pink china. For the women they had brought lipsticks and make-up, and they also carried a wind-up gramophone, for which the Bhutanese invented the word *ludrom,* meaning literally 'song box'. They didn't have to carry tents as camps made of bamboo and saplings were prepared for them at every stop, Granny describes '... a palatial camping ground – huts galore made of fir branches, kitchen, pantry, stables, several separate rooms for servants, each with its fire in the centre of the room (huge logs) and a delightful sitting room for us with bamboo seats'.

Above: Joan Mary, Granny, Grandpa and Revel Sinclair. Grandpa has a sort of proto-type bum-bag of extra pockets attached to a belt. Granny always wore hats at a theatrically rakish angle. The group, photographed by Dagmar, pose outside one of their specially-erected huts.
Left: Tea outside one of their bedrooms. The huts were decorated inside with carpets and silk wall hangings, often garlanded with rhododendrons: very different from our own more modest blue nylon tents.

Left: Nothing tastes sweeter than clean mountain stream water. The dwarf rhododendrons and azaleas behind me blaze into colour in the early spring. At this altitude ravens are our constant companions, but although the hills are home to leopards and blue sheep we never see them; probably they are scared off by our great procession of ponies and people.

Right: Maybe fishing in the ice-cold waters of a small lake; there are trout in these depths but she and Namgay never get a bite, which doesn't perturb them in the least. In the stillness, the only sound is that of Maybe's line spinning out.

From the moment they arrived in Bhutan the King sent baskets of food: butter, meat, rice, fresh fruit and vegetables, yak milk, fish sent from miles away. Raja Topgay Dorji was 'the world's most perfect host'. Topgay was thirty-four years old: apart from his position as *Deb Zimpön* of the state, he was Governor of the Ha district in western Bhutan, the first area the Weir expedition visited on its eastward-bound journey. There he had provided them with a lavish welcome, with mules and servants at their disposal and hospitality at his own private apartments in the fort. 'We had tea in his

chapel room. There was an altar in the corner, the usual butterlamps; and shields and swords decorated the painted walls. He took us through other rooms full of dried and drying yak and literally hundredweights of butter, some of it two years old. In this climate, like Tibet, butter lasts for years. It seemed incongruous having an English tea in these surroundings. Everything is on a gigantic scale here – and most generous.'

We are made no less welcome at each camp site. The little tents are pitched and blue mattresses, sometimes rather soggy from braving hailstorms on horseback, are placed inside each one. Tea, coffee and biscuits are always ready when we stumble up in the dusk, and from Mindu's tent waft gorgeous smells of supper cooking. The ponies and mules, released from their burdens, roll in the grass, grunting and squealing to each other before mooching off to graze nearby. The dunny, the lavatory tent, is pitched at a discreet distance, although some of us disappear behind rocks and bushes instead of entering its tiny confined space set over a deep hole. If you take a torch in with you at night-time, you can be seen in vivid silhouette.

Supper is immaculately served by Poba, who is the waiter. There is always far too much, but we know that what is left will be eaten by the rest of the men. No meal in Bhutan is complete without chillies – they have them even at breakfast, and every table has a dish of chilli sauce which is so hot that my eyes water in memory as I write. After supper, tea or coffee, hot-water bottles are put in our laps as we play liar dice. The Bhutanese are very keen on gambling games and are very good at them – Namgay takes to liar dice like a duck to water; luckily we're playing without real money or we'd all be paupers.

When we reach the second lake and the sun is setting we decide to film some outside bonfire footage. The chaps have constructed a huge pyre of rhododendron wood and we all gather round it turning lobster red in the blaze and listening to Nado telling slightly blue jokes in Bhutanese. There is much laughter and slapping of legs. Maybe is sitting next to a very old man who's nicknamed Kaka: she keeps him supplied with cigarettes and Nado says, 'They're getting married!' to hoots of laughter. There is no television in Bhutan (although there are a few privately owned videos) and people are still used to entertaining each other in the evenings.

For Granny and Grandpa the Paro Penlop had produced two court jesters: '... the snake man and the frog man, who played up nobly. I happened to mention a war dance. He immediately had a log fire built outside and sent for his warriors who did a most awe-inspiring dance in the moonlight. It was very beautiful and we were much impressed. We played the gramophone for a while and were conscious of faces and bodies pressing up against the matting walls, so keen was their interest in us. The Bhutanese are very musical...'.

The Paro Penlop wearing his dark red shoulder shawl, or kabné, and the Raven Crown, decorated with skull-faces still seen in the masks of today's dancers. Granny called him 'our dear little Paro Penlop... of whom we had grown so fond'. He provided them with all kinds of entertainment, notably a warriors' dance round a bonfire requested by Granny one night. Perhaps his un-Bhutanese shoes were a present from the Weirs. The Penlop had great artistic skills, and designed the beautiful palace at Paro where the Queen Mother now resides.

*Left: Glimpsed from a rocky pass, our camp site looks enviably attractive.
While we make our way more slowly, filming as we go, the porters travel on
ahead so that everything is prepared by the time we arrive in the evening.
Above: At night the temperature plummets to 13° below freezing, and frost
decorates not only the leaves and ferns but also ponies' manes, dogs' coats
and our underclothes drying on top of our tents.*

We haven't got a gramophone but we do have a CD player and some
songs from the 1930s. I ask one of the porter's sons to dance with me and
quite unabashed he takes my hand and I put his other round my waist and
we step solemnly in time on the frosty grass. His name is Tsentsay and he's
fifteen years old, but looks younger. The black dog wags his tail at us from
behind a tent, watching his master foxtrotting in the firelight and the moonlight with an older woman.

The next morning half the ponies have escaped from our valley, having found better grazing elsewhere – a perfect case of the grass being greener. We set off on foot with some of the camera gear being carried; this is excellent as I want to walk the whole way today anyway, right down to Thimphu, where we will be in a hotel for the night. There is a general air of jubilation that we've spent the last night under canvas for a short while... no more sleepless nights stuffed into sarcophagus-like sleeping bags with all your clothes on and still ending up frozen. We are the highest altitude yet – still only at 14,800 ft but that's about the same height as the summit of Mont Blanc. The paths are wide and stony and the views so spectacular that we decide to take a group photograph with the snowy peaks of Chomolhari behind us. Away to the north I glimpse another giant. 'What's that one, Namgay?' and I write down what it sounds like, Kan Kur Pinsum, which turns out to be GangKar Punsum, the highest mountain in Bhutan. Beyond lies Chinese-occupied Tibet. Tiny, independent, land-locked Bhutan lies between the colossal powers of India and China. It is only about the size of Switzerland, with 600,000 inhabitants or thereabouts. Books I've read on earlier political and trade missions describe how Bhutan lay across a vital route for merchandise from Bengal to Tibet, and how the Scot, George Bogle, an envoy from the Government of India, negotiated with Bhutan's head of temporal power, the *Deb Raja*, as long ago as 1774. There was no king in those days; instead, each region was administered by an overlord from his dzong. Until the early twentieth century, Bhutan was constantly suffering feuds and civil wars between rival penlops, brigands and barons, and border disputes with her neighbours, including the British in India and Sikkim. Peace and good relations were restored in the later nineteenth century, and in 1905 the Political Officer in Sikkim, John Claude White, was sent to invest the Tongsa Penlop, Ugyen Wangchuk, with the KCIE. In 1907 Sir Ugyen Wangchuk was chosen unanimously by lamas, headmen and the people of Bhutan as their hereditary Maharaja – the first King of Bhutan.

The fourth King, His Majesty Jigme Singye Wangchuk, is now on the throne. Before we left Paro, we had rather humbly sent him some presents, having been told that he was in religious retreat and that we wouldn't have the chance to give them personally. These wouldn't, of course, be rifles and ammunition or the grander presents usually sent by governments, but a token of the enduring friendship between our families over the years. Maybe and I had decided to frame a photograph of Grandpa and the King in their ceremonial robes. I visited the Queen's jeweller, Garrards, before we left London, and asked to be shown some beautiful frames. 'It's a present for a king,' I said. Without batting an eyelid the courteous assistant said, 'Which kingdom, Madam?' – a very cool rejoinder. The frame is made of solid gold and silver, and lapis lazuli, which always seems a regal stone, dark deep blue, bright-flecked with gold.

Now we're starting our descent to Thimphu and the film cameras want us riding again. At that moment, two beefy Europeans appear on foot, coming towards us. 'Look at you riding! I bet you'll make out you walked!' they yell and we give cheesy grins, trapped in the truth of their remark. There is cairn by the side of the path at the top of the hairpin route down. We put stones on it for Grandpa, Granny, Dagmar and Joan Mary, and all their valiant fellow travellers. Then we disentangle our bags from the ponies and start off downhill.

Chapter Six

The Heart of the Country

Around 5000 ft below and four hours later we totter like zombies on to level ground. The path has been relentlessly steep, past small dzongs and an occasional alpine pasture but mostly through dark pinewoods. It is well worn; we meet all kinds of tourists hiking to the top for the day. Some seem to be quite old: I can't think how they've got the strength in their thighs for this kind of walking, all of it with your feet pointing down like a medieval knight on a tomb. Some of these walkers are really cheerful too: 'Hey! Good to know you! Whoah! It's tough!'. Because my boots are slightly too big for me, I've put on two thick pairs of socks, but my big toes push agonizingly against the ends. The boots were given to me by the army when I was sent off to live on a desert island for nine days. They were too hot and too big then, but on this trip they've served me very well and I'm used to seeing policeman-sized feet flinging out in front of me. As days go by on

There are still no roads in many of the heavily wooded valleys.
The people who live here have their own paths and ways but from a distance
the hills roll away forever, looking completely uninhabited. Occasionally
one glimpses a meadow which means cultivation of crops or pasture.

these expeditions favourite clothes emerge: a specially soft cotton shirt, a good waxed waistcoat, a comfortable handkerchief for the neck, a nice hat to keep the hot and cold at bay. The boots were once firm friends – now I have my doubts as I'm completely lame.

The ponies and mules have gone ahead of us and soon vanish from view down the stony ladder of the hill. We never see them again. We've given parting gifts of baseball caps to the porters (an especially nice one for my dance partner Tsentsay) and they seem pleased and put them on when they change from mountain clothes to their smart city ghos before they enter the capital. They speed away from us, and many of them will go on to other treks (what few there are), and our little community will be dispersed. At the end of any group venture, when you've all shared the same experience, it's a wrench to let go and say goodbye, and realize that everyone has a home to go to. Easy come, easy go: it's quite a lesson to try to absorb. Some of us never learn it by heart.

We sing cheerful songs on the way down as dusk falls but the Thimphu Valley seems to recede rather than draw closer in the gloaming. By the time we get to the bottom we are silent, having left the rushes-o growing greenly far behind. A Jeep has arrived to pick us up and take us to the Druk Hotel. Lots of things in Bhutan are called Druk, which means dragon. Bhutan itself is called Druk Yul, the Land of the Thunder Dragon, a name of immeasurable splendour. The Druk Hotel is very well appointed, reminding us of skiing lodges in Europe – wood-panelled rooms with shutters and a pleasant dining-room with a bar. We are on the fourth floor without a lift, and this short upward journey now becomes almost unbearable as our muscle-thickened legs begin to set. We arrive like Frankenstein's monsters in the bar for some excellent beer and peanuts. Captain George, our pilot-hero, is there, his moustache larger than ever and his attractive American girlfriend on his arm. He has almost become an honorary Bhutanese citizen: he has a house here, loves the life, is looked after like royalty by his superb house servant and can't see any point in changing anything. He is infectiously good-humoured – people always say, 'Oh, *we* flew in with Captain George,' as if they had been transported personally by the Angel Gabriel. From some sort of sound system in the bar I hear *Lohengrin* and 'O mio babbino caro', which remind me so sharply of my husband Stephen I nearly blub. Homesickness can jump up at you like a hammer sometimes: it hits you hard on the head and then vanishes. It always comes, but then it always goes. Upstairs later, the hot bath takes hours to run but is blissful. I rub Deep Heat into my knees and feet (knowing it's too late) and inspect my toenails: they have turned black. The room is dark-panelled and is now strewn with shirts and socks that need washing. Clothes have a way of cleaning themselves on trips: if you fold them up neatly enough, they are as good as new in a couple of days. I finished Anthony Powell's *The Valley of Bones* last night in the tent. Now I hardly have time to open *A Time of Gifts* by Patrick Leigh Fermor before Morpheus seizes me in his sleepy embrace and drags me towards strange dreams.

'*Tsongkhang gatimo?*' means where is the nearest shop, but in Thimphu I don't have to ask, as there are two before you even leave the hotel. We can see that money will be flying out of our purses; everything is just what I want and pretty much identical to the treasures Granny and Grandpa brought back with them. The town is charming – very busy and bustling with traffic

directed by a policeman whose arm movements are astonishing and balleti-
cally graceful. People throng the pavements; women and young girls with
babies slung across their backs and fronts in papoose-type shawls, smart
executives in grey ghos with black shoes and brogues, lamas in red and
orange robes, small urchins asking for pens but not begging for money.
Begging is looked down on in Bhutan; although some of the people seem to
be extremely poor, no one starves and even the animals are well fed and
healthy. The architecture is entrancing. No shop or house is too small for
elaborate carving and painting in rich colours. The wood-shingled roofs are
sometimes replaced by yellow-painted corrugated iron (noisy when the rain
falls). There is a government policy that Bhutan shall retain at least 65 per
cent of its virgin Himalayan forest, and forestry is of enormous national
importance as all the new, old-looking houses are principally made of
pinewood. Although Thimphu looks as old as time, it wasn't here when the
Weir expedition came through. It consisted only of the colossal Tashichho
Dzong (the Fortress of Auspicious Religion), and a few rustic houses. Now
it's the centre of government, and the King's throne room lies in the heart
of the dzong. Thirty-four thousand citizens buzz about the streets under

*The gorgeously decorated roof of one of the temples in the Tashichho Dzong
in Thimphu, where pigeons wheel and settle to the drone of ceaseless prayers.
The dzong has been burned down several times but each time like a perfect
phoenix it rises up, looking not only much the same but also larger and grander
too. Inside this temple is a two-storey-sized Buddha whose top half reaches into
the second floor. Even temples have open-air lofts where food can be wind-
dried. All the painting is kept looking fresh and bright: it's very hard to know
how old any building is, as they're all built to the traditional regulations.*

the burning blue of the sky. High on the hillside above the great majestic shape of the dzong stands a wild forest of prayer flags, more than you can count: 'Continuous as the stars that shine, And twinkle on the Milky Way, They stretch'd in never-ending line...' showering blessings down on the palaces of the King and his four queens, and the homes and shops of their loyal subjects. There is a cinema, showing mainly Hindi films, and an excellent Swiss bakery built like a circular chalet, from which good coffee and bread smells drift out.

These are the things I buy: a basket-weave suitcase, some old coins, two prayer wheels like babies' rattles, wooden prayer-printing blocks, wild silk prayer shawls in oxblood and ivory, *paan* and lime boxes for the preparation of betel nuts, a kira, some wooden masks, bracelets, a jacket and blouse, and a *koma* – the Celtic-looking brooches worn one on each shoulder of the kira and linked by a chain. I've seen these in portrayals of imaginary Celtic folk and I think I've also seen them at the Victoria and Albert Museum, the self-same brooches and chains. How can they be so similar? But many of the colours here are very like those loved in Latin America – and Mexico is, amazingly, on the same line of latitude as Bhutan. Perhaps some notions of dress and custom waft like thistledown over the Earth, settling in and twinning unlinked locations.

Inside a clothing shop with carved casements I try on a gho to see if it will be the right size for Stephen or Jamie, my son. They're all lined with cornflower-blue cotton and are mostly made of checked or striped wool or cotton. Small boys giggle through the window at such an absurd sight – a woman in a man's robe! – and a browsing lama looks at me critically and nods kindly but I think he's only being polite.

*Above: Struggling to tie myself into a gho to see if it will fit Jamie,
my son who's 6´ 2˝. The standard of craftsmanship here is very high, and a
shopping spree can seriously damage your wallet as you fill bags with silver,
silk and wooden ornaments, both old and new. These onlookers are laughing
quite loudly at the sight of me in men's clothes; I must look quite
ridiculous to them even though I'm feeling* très chic.
*Overleaf: Two little girls gaze at me in amazement. Maybe has brought with
her an excellent assortment of pens and pencils which make nice presents
for these small schoolchildren.*

'It's not for ladies,' says the shopkeeper anxiously and I act out 'husband' for him by showing my wedding ring and assuming an expression of great happiness. How could we in Europe dress to look shocking any more, we who wear men's trousers and coats, building-site boots, see-through blouses, high-heeled gym shoes and lycra leggings? With the gho neatly stashed on top of our enormous bag of goods, we clomp back to the Druk Hotel for turnips and chick-pea curry.

We've asked to see some archery, if anyone is having a contest that day, about as dim an enquiry as asking if football is played on Saturdays anywhere in Britain. At once we are whisked off in cars to a beautiful estate outside the town belonging to Colonel Rinzing, late of the king's bodyguard, who remembers the 1931 expedition.

'Your grandfather was a good friend to Bhutan,' he said, offering cakes and tea. The two targets are about 140 yards apart and just happen to straddle a deep gully and small wood. The bull's-eye is hardly visible to me but the colonel's first arrow goes thwunk! straight into the centre and his team start a slow dance of victory with cries of triumph and pitying jeers. Each team is supported by cheerleaders, an attractive bunch of young women who stand in line beside their team member, crooning seductively to help his aim, but chanting appalling insults to the opponents.

'I can't translate them all, actually,' says Namgay. 'They're pretty rude, mostly about people's appearance.'

'Like what?'

'Like: you are as bald as a turnip and have a face like a pig's bottom, that kind of thing.'

The Bhutanese are champion archers but didn't fire their best shots when they took part in the Olympics. Perhaps it was because they found the competition rather... well... uncompetitive. Here they stand right in front of the target as their opponent takes aim, yelling and hooting, and the pretty girls sing and you have to make allowance for the breeze and so forth. Until quite recently their bows and arrows were real weapons with poisoned tips, used against each other, and for hunting wild boar, deer and leopard. Some are still using bamboo bows, although a few steel contraptions have crept in: most despised are the telescopic sights, which they consider take the fun and skill out of the sport. As we watch, you couldn't put a pin between them today and their predecessors sixty-five years ago, captured on camera with their dancing and laughing and firing. You can almost make out Raja Topgay Dorji, watching from the shadows and taking an arrow from his quiver in the flickering black and white film of February 1931.

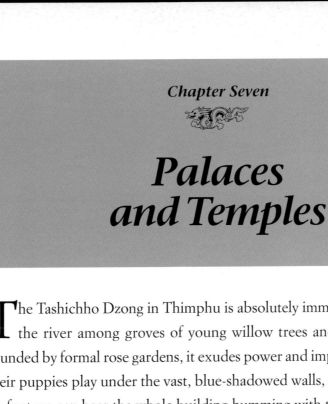

Chapter Seven

Palaces and Temples

The Tashichho Dzong in Thimphu is absolutely immense. Spread out by the river among groves of young willow trees and poplars, and surrounded by formal rose gardens, it exudes power and importance. Dogs with their puppies play under the vast, blue-shadowed walls, and as we approach on foot we can hear the whole building humming with the chants of monks at morning devotion. It's on such a grand scale that we're dwarfed by the first giant staircase which will take us up past the security officers standing at a low table, where mighty prayer wheels the size of colossal oil drums spin and ring. In the eaves above us doves croon and flutter. We've put on smartish gear, arms covered, heads bare, as we're entering a holy place which is also the centre of government and the King's Offices – rather like Westminster Abbey and the House of Commons rolled up with Buckingham Palace. Special permission has been sent for us to visit.

To stand near the walls of the Tashichho Dzong is to understand its size. Because the windows start so high up it feels like a castle from outside. The vast courtyards inside are at about the second or third storey. This dzong is now the centre of spiritual and temporal power in Bhutan: official groups and government cars come and go all day. Women may never be within a dzong after sunset.

As with many dzongs in Bhutan, this one allows visitors only at certain times – many more dzongs are closed to the outside world and women are never allowed to be inside the walls after sunset. The marble staircase is gold and umber, dark after the glare of the sun: the guard nods permission and we start on up to the sound of deep-throated chanting, booming, bells and horns sounding, a huge blanket of sound bombing from wall to wall... then, suddenly, we are in the central courtyard which is so enormous that we gasp aloud. The ground is smoothly paved with grey slabs covering the size of two football pitches. Buildings with verandas, cloisters and shallow steps enclose the space; and although all the brickwork is painted lime white, the overall effect from the fantastic, intricately painted carved wood is of blazing colour. It's as clean as a whistle – not a leaf or a scrap of paper blows. Minute figures hurry to and fro on errands, each with the *kabné*, their shoulder scarf, slung diagonally across their robes – white for commoners, red and white in panels for village headmen and some lay priests, and dark red for men of senior rank. The monks are also in red – in shades that drift from scarlet to rust – talking in groups, standing by the wall of small prayer wheels, collecting fresh water for the orange marigolds, the temple flowers. There are refectories, classrooms, temples, dormitories, state rooms, each area grander than

---

Sometimes a building catches at your heart it is so perfect.
The size of this huge structure can be judged by the shiny steep staircase
rising to the second floor. This is the oldest building within the Tashichho
Dzong and my favourite building of all time. The French have a word for it:
mondiale, *world class. Being foreign visitors, we aren't allowed to get any*
closer than this as the pavement in front is out-of-bounds to us.
We're content to gape at its beauty from afar.

Above: Wood painting in Bhutan is as common a craft as concrete mixing is in the west. Soon we recognise the traditional emblems and motifs; the colours are rich and bold within the formality of the designs. The carving itself is intricate; the finished result is dazzling. The painting both inside and outside temples is especially detailed.

Right: In Bhutan, many families send one son to the monastery to keep alive the Buddhist faith and tradition. Boys start as young as six and although most of them stay within the order for the rest of their lives, one or two drop out in their late teens. They thrive on comradeship and discipline and they have to learn scripture, wash their own clothes, work hard and not be cheeky (or a senior lama will flick them with a long whip). Many learn a few English phrases, which they politely try out on visitors like us.

the last. One building there stops your breath: it has a two-storey approach up outside steps and soaring lattice-work casements reaching up to a free-standing roof. All roofs seem to have open lofts: not only these great dzong buildings, but also humble village houses. They're used for storage of food and household things, and for air-drying vegetables and meat.

I can't tell how long we stand and wander and stare. Suddenly the chant-ing stops and through a pagoda-type entrance to one temple comes a long procession of monks headed by the Chief Abbot in a rich yellow kabné. Only he and the King may wear this royal colour. (I am suddenly reminded of the Raja of Sarawak, who many miles away and many years ago always walked under a yellow umbrella.) In front of the Chief Abbot, a monk, bowing slightly, slow-handclaps the progress. The Abbot looks at us and we bow, then he strides off across the courtyard with the rest of the monks filing out after him in order of age and seniority. Bringing up the rear are really tiny boys, some of them only seven or eight years old.

Three great prayer wheels, the size of oil drums, spinning in the loggia before the entrance to the Tashichho Dzong. Each wheel has a bell above it which rings at each revolution. Part of the Buddhist tradition too are prayer beads, or rosaries, used for exactly the same purpose. Chanting a familiar prayer is common to many religions: one of the reasons for the objections to new translations of Christian prayers and bibles is that the familiar chant or mantra, stretching unchanged through the centuries, is broken. 'Om mani padme hum' repeated over and over becomes a kind of blur of sound; rather like someone saying a hundred 'Hail Marys'. Above the wheels, impervious to the noise and bustle below, roost the temple doves on lavishly carved beams, cooing and rustling to each other before taking off for a tour of inspection in the dzong courtyards.

Leaning on the pagoda I try to make a drawing of the detailed windows. There is a heavy breathing at my shoulder: some small monks are looming over me, watching every line I make.

'I'll draw you,' I say, and after some pushing and shoving among them, an eleven-year-old poses gracefully, leaning on the balustrade and gazing at me unwinkingly for a couple of minutes.

'What's your name?'

'Chimi Dorji.'

'*Kadinche la*, Chimi Dorji, thank you very much.'

The small boys rush off with yells of glee, quickly shepherded in by an older monk. Some carry big whips which they smack on the ground to herald a lama, or just to give the boys the odd flick to keep order.

Namgay is talking to an official beside the main temple, nodding and gesticulating. Somehow he has gained permission for us to enter the shrine and have a brief look round. We leave our shoes on the veranda outside and

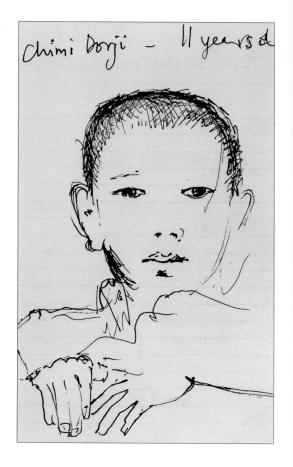

Whereas people sometimes feel self-conscious when they're being photographed (and in some countries cameras represent the evil eye) no one seems to mind being drawn. I only have my notebook with me and a black pen, but the boys who watch me drawing Chimi Dorji think my sketch looks fine.

80

step into the room. The floor is highly polished, probably by the thousands of bodies who've sat on the broad dark floorboards. There are oil lamps and candles and butterlamps, and in the thin shafts of sunlight we can see the two-storey figure of Buddha, his head and shoulders quite out of sight, being upstairs in the floor above. The walls on each side are entirely covered with glass-fronted cases, each containing an identical figure of Buddha about 18 inches high. I do rapid calculations and come to 956 ('A thousand,' says Namgay). Each Buddha wears a gold shawl. There are thangkas and columns of silk, altar-cloths, mounds of rice, dishes of water, marigolds, paintings of saints and deities, every single thing having an important religious meaning. Outside on the veranda walls are large depictions of wheels of life and *mandalas*, representing the universe and mankind's complicated journey from birth to death and beyond. Mandalas can also be made of sand, in the same geometrical and circular form, and dedicated to particular deities. They take three weeks to make, the coloured, flour-fine sand being pain-stakingly poured into the most intricate designs. On an appointed day a ceremony will be held and after this *puja* the mandala will be spoilt by a single stroke of a finger and thrown into the river to demonstrate the impermanence of all things. In fact, impermanence is inherent in the Thimphu Dzong, as it has been burned down and rebuilt many times. It all looks ancient, however, and as permanent as the hills that surround it. This is the summer residence for the monks. When winter comes, the whole community will pack up and migrate to their winter lodgings at Punakha, which is at a lower altitude and has a much milder climate.

At the hotel, Ashi Kendum Dorji has arrived with a maid and brought up to my room piles of superb kiras and fine jewellery. *Ashi*, loosely translated,

means 'The Lady' and she is the granddaughter of Grandpa's host and friend Raja Topgay Dorji. She is extremely pretty with creamy skin, small white hands and flashing brown eyes. She is also a formidable businesswoman, world traveller and sophisticate. We are invited for dinner tonight at her family home and we all think it would be rather good if Maybe and I went in traditional Bhutanese dress. Kiras are kept packed flat, like saris. Kendum's kiras are extraordinarily grand and valuable: some belonged to her grand-mother, some she has had woven to her own design. We stand in front of the looking-glass holding up first one, then another. We choose two which will suit us, in singing colours of turquoise, cream, green and pink, woven so delicately that they look like silk embroidery. Kiras are passed down from generation to generation, as the finest are worn only on high days and holidays. It's just beginning to be fashionable again, to wear granny's kira – the cool kids had moved into a phase of machine-made kiras in imported fabrics, but now the wheel has turned full circle and rather like us digging out devoré velvet opera jackets, the old stuff has swung back in to hold its own. The jewellery is tremendously weighty – open-sided bracelets, heavy

Mahayana Buddhism is a most intricately structured religion, with many deities, saints, manifestations, goddesses and symbols. Inside a Buddhist temple are so many images that the eyes and mind are overwhelmed. The beauty of the paintings and carvings, the splendour of the silk hangings and the delicacy of moulded butterlamps present a feast of colour and activity. Offerings of food and dishes of water are laid out daily on the altars, and religious devotions are carried out from dawn to dusk. Religion is a central part of Bhutanese life, as normal and engrossing there as television has become in the western world.

necklaces, the *koma* brooches with suspended chain, a rather unwieldy head ornament which I foolishly agree to wear, pearl and turquoise earrings, a ring as big as a matchbox. The maid shows us how to put the clothes on, but we will have to be helped later on in the evening when we dress properly.

Packing for two months' rough travelling followed by a grand cere-monial occasion must have presented some problems for Granny and Joan Mary. I don't think they were obsessively clean (any more than we are) and their outer day clothes would have withstood all kinds of hardships. They wore jodhpurs, boots or strong walking shoes, vests and blouses, waistcoats made from material woven in the Swat Valley on the Northwest Frontier of India, good brimmed hats (Granny's always worn at a rakish angle), ties, belts, stout woollen socks. Grandpa had a sort of prototype bum-bag: extra pockets suspended from a belt and worn over his breeks.

I wish I could remember him: he died when I was three years old, and I have only one photograph of us together, me sitting on his lap in Hong Kong. He and Granny eventually retired to Kenya where they built a house at Karen, outside Nairobi. He had the brightest blue eyes and a keen sense of humour: everyone who knew him loved him, not least the people who worked with him. The young doctor, Lieutenant Revel Sinclair, went with him on several trips. Together they made a dashing pair, particularly when they wore their richly coloured *ghos.* Sinclair sometimes wore shorts and they all had thick, home-knitted jerseys to keep out the cold. They had fur coats, deerstalker hats, tweeds, mufflers and night-clothes, all worn, or packed away in baskets and gunny bags on the ponies' backs. Even in an hotel it's difficult to get clothes laundered quickly; moving on from day to day, camp to camp, means, in our case, underclothes freezing to cardboard

Even though it was mid-winter Lieutenant Sinclair, the medical officer, often wore shorts and socks. In those days travellers favoured stout shoes, like Granny's, which were kept well polished (though probably not by her). At her feet is one of the four dogs they took with them: with all the porters' hounds as well, the animals galloping along would have made up what was called a 'bobbery pack'.

as they're spread out on top of the tents, and socks fluttering dry from the windows of Jeeps. I imagine they had a similar system going then, but they would never have had the luxury of a hot bath.

Granny and Dagmar would always have been 'properly turned out', with hair dressed neatly (in Granny's case plaited into earphones) and lipstick on. Joan Mary didn't wear any make-up, as Grandpa mentioned earlier. She had huge blue eyes and blonde hair and was already a notable beauty. Aware of the progressively potato-like appearance of my own face, I've worn lipstick and mascara every day for the cameras, to try to look a bit sparky. Both Maybe and I slap on sunblock to stop us frizzling to a crisp but it doesn't seem to give us much of a headstart over the forebears, who didn't have anything other than Pond's Cold Cream. Dagmar, who had joined the Weir expedition from Singapore, was considered to be 'a bit soft for the journey, in poor shape', but compared with us she survived like an athlete in training. Granny and Joan Mary had taken with them four dogs: one had puppies on the trip, which were put into a wicker basket and carried carefully for the whole journey. Their expedition must have been immeasurably different in many ways, and so similar in others. Here in Thimphu we can fax or phone home, tune in to the news, buy a slightly out-of-date newspaper, catch an aeroplane; but because of the Driglam Namzha regulations, which preserve the national identity of Bhutan in traditional customs, dress and architecture, we feel like travellers in an antique land.

We are getting dressed for the dinner party. It takes some time to get used to being put into clothes by the maid, odder for Maybe than for me, as in the film and theatre world one is always being hauled in and out of alien garments. First, a petticoat and the vivid shawl-collared silk blouse with very long sleeves; then the kira itself is folded, pinned, draped, positioned and tied so it becomes a long sleeveless tunic, tightly belted and bloused at the waist. Then a short brocade jacket is slipped on and the blouse sleeves roll back with the jacket sleeves to make deep cuffs. The etiquette concerning clothes in Bhutan is strict, particularly with the length of the gho, the man's tunic – only the King may cover his knees and the humblest people must wear the hem above the knee. The length of the cuff is important too: the deeper it is, the higher your social standing. The gho, like the kira, is bloused at the waist, creating a capacious pocket into which chaps can stow almost anything from wallets and paan boxes to daggers and eating bowls. This accounts for the rather portly look in photographs of otherwise lean, fit men.

Kendum's family house is full of friends: among them Kendum's cousin, the urbane Dasho Benjy Dorji, another of Raja Topgay Dorji's grandchildren, welcoming us with brimming glasses of champagne. *Dasho* is a title, somewhere between Sir and Prince. In his report to the Indian Government, Grandpa used the old spelling *Trashö* when he wrote of the King's younger brothers. Benjy is a nickname, his real name being Paljor. We talk of conservation, the Black-necked cranes, racing at Newmarket, and we eat wild orchids and red rice, a local speciality. The room is highly decorated in orange, blue, gold, and green, like sitting in a jewel box. Maybe is talking to Ashi Tashi, the Queen Mother's sister, a tiny and dynamic figure brimming over with affection and fun. They are deep in quiet conversation, talking about Joan Mary and catching up on family news. I feel a bit unwieldy in my kira, like a rolled-up carpet, but Kendum says, 'You look very nice.' She wears her blouse folded slightly lower round the throat and looks serene and elegant. My head decoration is moving about a bit and I am aware that I'm the only person wearing one. The belt, tied by the maid as though I were a dangerous prisoner, is cutting me in half.

'It's wonderful when you take it off at the end of the day,' says Kendum. 'You can feel your food going down at last.'

Chapter Eight

Gateway to the East

'Bhutan' wrote Grandpa 'is a country roughly rectangular, which runs some 200 miles from east to west, and 100 miles from north to south.' Tongsa, our next stop, is about half-way up and half-way along, in fact almost right in the middle of Bhutan. We now drive along the Thimphu to Tashigang Highway, an engineering miracle of a road which creeps and claws its way round precipitous gorges, following the contours of the hills and providing views to knock your hat off. Waterfalls dash down steep stony cliffs, little orchids grasping the stony ground wave out above our heads. Sometimes we pass grazing yak herds, their odd thick tails clumped behind them and long, shovel-shaped faces raised to look at us with irritation as we zim by. The distant valleys are beautifully terraced for rice, barley and buckwheat. The river snakes along the valley bed, shallow, swift-running and glittering. Most of the old bridges Granny loved have gone now, having

---

Skillfully terraced fields lie along the valleys below the Thimphu–
Tashigang highway. All the crops are cut by hand; buckwheat, barley and rice.
Round the Paro region, red rice is the common staple. Pale pink when
cooked, it has a delicious unusual flavour.

either fallen down or been replaced by modern steel girders. Often we slow to a halt as sheep are driven ahead of us. Everyone we pass waves. These are long hard days in the Jeep, when you're itching to be out walking or riding. We will break our journey for lunch at the Wangdi-Phodrang Dzong. By now, the Weirs had been travelling for thirteen days. Granny's diary recalls:

'Our journey to Wangdi-Phodrang soon brought us to a lovely dry pine country with reddish grass undergrowth. Bright blue berries everywhere, like elder. Our road was high up above the river and before very long we spied blue sheep, about six, in the distance in steep, rocky country. Rounding the next corner, we came into full view of the lovely monastery just above the junction of two rivers. Below the fort stands a beautiful wooden bridge. Strange growths of enormous cactus covered the hill below the dzong. These are probably prickly pears, literally smothered with fruit, some very red in colour and bearing prickles. I believe people feed them to the cattle.'

The plateau where their camp was built was high up behind the dzong, 'not far from a pretty clump of fir trees'. Now we are sitting by the trees on the plateau, watched by curious-eyed children whose mothers are washing things by the village pump. There are very few houses, and several prayer flags are flapping furiously in the stiff breeze. 'Wind made sketching impossible,' wrote Granny. 'It rather spoilt our pleasure. It raged fiercely until sunset and altered our desire to stay here for two or three extra days.' Instead they made an excursion to Punakha, about an 8-mile journey for them, 'a lovely ride on a perfect morning'.

Punakha used to be the ancient capital of Bhutan, situated in a sub-tropical valley of great beauty and fertility. Soon the monk community will be arriving there. They were in residence in the winter of January 1931:

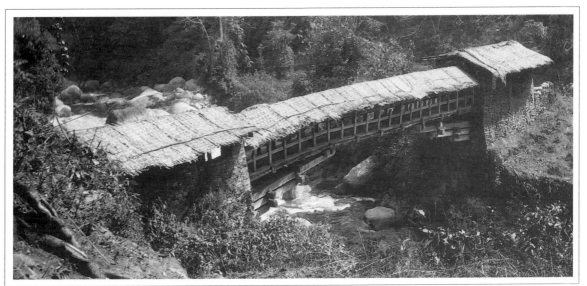

Most of the old bridges that Granny loved are now gone;
luckily we have photographs and drawings to remember them by.
Overleaf: Her beautiful pastel drawing of Punakha Dzong.

'... and the lamas showed us great courtesy. An orange tree in full fruit in a
huge pot almost entirely filled one of the small courtyards. The usual picturesque bridge spanned the river and the bank below the dzong was
encased in a solid wall.' Granny's pastel drawing of the dzong shows the
wonderful cantilevered covered bridge. She was self-taught as an artist,
inspired by stupendous Tibetan monasteries and the Potala Palace in Lhasa.
Her buildings really sit on the ground, the walls are thick and windows
deep. She loved the clean sharp colours of the sky against the ochre, rust and
white of the structures. Joan Mary had the gift of portraiture, capturing
people exactly. Even as a seventeen-year-old her talent was remarkable.

Although I have brought crayons and pastels with me, I end up making only a few measly pencil and ink scrawls, slightly letting the side down. But I've brought my lovely, rather labour-intensive camera and lenses, and Maybe is keeping up the tradition of filming on her video camera. Drawing something, however, tends to make it stick in your mind for longer. It's as though one were learning with every stroke made. Many actors learn their lines by writing them out, like homework.

Before we leave our picnic site near the Wangdi-Phodrang Dzong, we ask Namgay to distribute some of the pens and pencils we've brought with us as presents. The children line up politely in front of him, each receiving their gift with both hands outstretched. In Bhutan you give and take with both hands and a slight bow. They are delighted and we feel ashamed that we haven't been able to bring more presents.

Long ago the doctor, Lieutenant Sinclair, performed small operations at impromptu surgeries held at each camp site, and administered 370 vaccinations. 'We have on record the treatment of 1343 new cases, but the number probably exceeded this figure owing to the fact that, with so limited a staff, efficient clerical work could not be carried out simultaneously with examination, diagnosis and treatment of a seething crowd, all giving their various symptoms at the same time and in a foreign language. Medical equipment consisted of a medical and a surgical pannier, and two large boxes containing bottles of ready-made mixtures and other necessary drugs. On the march, first-aid essentials and smallpox vaccine were carried in saddle-bags.' Nowadays, Bhutan has a free health service, free schooling for all and cheap electricity, with the hydro-electric systems generating enough to supply India as well.

*In the gloaming, the great Chendebji chorten looks quite out of
this world. Just below the central tower you can see one of the four pairs of
eyes, watching our every move. It was too dark to see the rickety bridge the
Weir expedition used – perhaps it has vanished. The trees have now
grown tall, making it even darker.*

There's a long drive ahead. By the time we reach Chendebji and its huge
chorten it's too dark to film. In the twilight the colossal monument sits like a
grand meringue 'built in the same way as the ones at Kathmandu' observed
Granny. Stone steps lead us to where the chorten stands, just below the road,
very ancient and exciting. Buried inside these shrines are gifts to the gods, of
wheat, rice and gold wrapped in silk. Above Chendebji the Jeeps wait in
silence as we walk round, clockwise, to the long mani wall on a well-used
path. At the top of the shrine four pairs of baleful eyes stare out at the four
corners of the valley, one pair on each side, watching travellers coming and

going. Although it has broad sides, all snowy white, there's not a mark on it, not one name scrawled or any aerosol artwork. In fact, there's no graffiti in Bhutan at all. It is extremely creepy being watched by a shrine. We hurry back to the vehicles and on to Tongsa.

We arrive long after dark. There is no moon tonight but we know we are above the dzong, staying at the delightful Sherubling Guest House, with wooden floors, wood-burning stoves and supper laid out for us. A small collection of kiras, ghos and scarves are laid out on a sofa, in case we want to buy something before we turn in. (We do.) The sofas themselves are covered with colourful woven cloths. Vases hold flowers from the gardens – zinnias, roses and marigolds – and candles glimmer on low tables. I would like to live here. In the dark and holding a key the size of soup spoon, I make my way to my little room, a bungalow away from the hotel, precariously positioned on a steep bank, or, indeed, a sheer drop. There are two beds, a candle and a picture of the King: the walls are made of beautifully plaited and woven bamboo. My bathroom is a no-nonsense affair: a cold tap, bucket, basin and lavatory on a plain earth floor. The lavatory is a 'long-drop', really just a seat over a hole in the ground. By candlelight I read of the camp that greeted my grandparents and Joan Mary. In many ways I'm staying in one of their rooms. 'Matting huts had been built and floored with proper planks (no saws available so all planks are hewn with axes – great work). A large reception room was hung with priceless thangkas. Our sleeping rooms were well equipped. Some of us had modern tents, very up-to-date ones from India. The doctor was provided with a large Bhutan tent lined with a delicate shade of pink flannelette – most heavenly glow. The windows of the main guest house were remarkable, being made of a most ingenious arrangement of grass matting. This slid along, allowing opening and shutting of windows. We were very happy here...' And so am I, with my book and alarm clock, thick woven blankets and bright candlelight to read by. The clock is set for five thirty a.m., I want to see the dzong by the light of the dawn.

It is absolutely massive, straggling down on many different levels, on a promontory of land beyond which are the steep, densely wooded gorges where the old road was. Ravens are wheeling round its yellow-painted roofs, so many surfaces that I lose count at fourteen. When the Weir expedition embarked on its journey, Tongsa Dzong was generally expected to be the site of the investiture ceremony. This used to be the Royal Family's ancestral winter residence, an impregnable fortress right in the centre of the country. However, when they arrived, plans had been changed and the King had decided that the investiture would take place in the most spiritual temple in Bhutan, the Kurjey Lhakhang in Bumthang in the east. The holiness of that temple cannot be exaggerated. Padmasambhava, Guru Rinpoche, who is said to have brought Buddhism to Bhutan, rested against a rock in the Bumthang Valley while he was preaching and an imprint of his body, a dent in the rock, remains to this day, covered over by a shrine. Kurjey literally means 'impression left by sacred body of Guru Rinpoche'.

Maybe and I walk down the zigzagging road to the dzong: the old route was straight up from the river '... a very steep ascent, rising about 1000 feet in three-quarters of a mile. Many monks came out in their full regalia, incense burners and trumpeters heralding our arrival. The steps up were very precipitous... we eventually rode through eerie gateways to a sunny

Above: The King's younger brothers in 1931, Dasho Dorji (left) and Dasho Nacku, aged nineteen and twelve respectively. Dasho Dorji welcomed the Weir party to Tongsa and young Dasho Nacku greeted them with hot tea on the final high cold pass before Bumthang. Sadly, Dasho Dorji died of typhoid fever when he was only twenty-two and Dasho Nacku also died of an illness when he was about thirty-two.
Right: The impressive steps leading up to the main entrance to Tongsa Dzong. In the old days it was the only route from east to west Bhutan.

colourful courtyard full of gaily clad lamas... we were entertained to a Bhutanese lunch; they had borrowed some tinned fruit and tinned cream to give it an English finishing touch. The hospitality was incredible.' Large baskets of fruit and pastries had been reaching them daily, sent from the King, and at Tongsa there were more than ever. By now they had been joined by Dasho Dorji, a younger brother of the King, who had been deputed to welcome them, '... a delightful lad, about nineteen years old, of good manners and great charm'.

Outside the dzong we wait in a small rose garden until Namgay joins us. Terraces of flower-beds follow a path down to below the dzong's walls on the left, where goats graze and a small bamboo bridge crosses a stream. Handsome chickens cluck and scratch in the grass and some small monks are carrying firewood. Ducking through a narrow doorway, we go in. It is quite unlike the Thimphu Dzong, being composed of smallish courtyards, joined by flights of whitewashed stone steps. Above us, jostling for room, the roofs almost touch and overlap, their beautiful carved beams freshly painted; small faces look out of windows, a lama pauses to nod at us, the distant drone of chanting floats from an unseen temple room. We go down and up and along, and rather like being in some fantastic Escher drawing we never quite seem to get anywhere. These secluded public courtyards seem to me to be just about perfectly constructed for town-house developments. They are slightly higgledy-piggledy, very grand, with terraces to lean on, stairs to sit on, windows to watch from. Some are small attic rooms (suitable for students), others larger (for big families) or nearer the ground (for older people and the handicapped), some with railings round them for mothers with scurrying toddlers. It's very depressing the way we build blocks of flats with identical amenities: when you're eighteen you don't want a family flat, and when you're old you want to be able to see life from your window. People get richer and poorer in their lives – a young married couple might prefer to live in a cramped one-bedroom flat and spend their money on travel, whereas people who work from home would give anything for some extra space for an office.

The sunlight in the courtyard is very hot and bright, the atmosphere is stifling. For some reason the place is overpowering and I begin to feel haunted. We enter a narrow, dark corridor with windows looking down to the green valley far below. I seem to be suffocating. Namgay is talking, telling us of the history. We are walking in this dark corridor along the only route from eastern Bhutan to the west. In the old days, the road ran up to the dzong, went up the steps, along this corridor and out into the courtyards we've just left. Granny and Grandpa, Joan Mary, Dagmar and Lieutenant Sinclair all walked through here with the King's brother Dasho Dorji, and as we walk forward their shadows pass through us on their older journey. Then, suddenly, we are in another bright yard and small monks are washing their robes with bars of soap at a pump; we're in the boys-only section of the monastery, so Maybe and I must turn back.

At the Sherubling Guest House Maybe and I are trying to work out exactly where our grandparents' camp site was. The dzong housed men only, and the royal ladies lived in a house of their own, a few hundred yards away. The camp was built very near to the ladies' quarters and once again winds rushing up the valleys, speckled with snowflakes, made the forebears tug their coats tightly round them. There is a round-turreted watch-tower high on the hill above the monastery, and, just below, the village. Tongsa is lovely,

Tongsa Dzong sprawls down the steep hillside with lookouts on all sides.
It was built without any drawings and assembled only using wooden dowels
and dovetailing. Its tin roofs glinting above shifting shadows seem like metallic
lime leaves. Each time we see a new dzong we swear it is the loveliest yet:
Wangdi-Phodrang, Tashichho, Paro… but Tongsa takes the prize so far.

a busy pronged road with single-storey houses at street level, but behind them, as the cliff falls away, we see rooms underneath, and walkways and balconies. On a small green beside the road, boys are throwing darts with deadly accuracy and each bull's-eye is greeted with howls of triumph. A lorry gasps through at 3 miles an hour, black smoke belching from its exhaust pipe, more noticeable here because the air is so very clean, sweet and unpolluted. Woodsmoke, spices and incense are the usual scents hanging in the air.

'I wish we could find some juniper,' says Maybe. 'All the welcoming fires were made of juniper, but if you were very poor you just burned a small heap of any old leaves or pine needles.' We look around vaguely at the trees and realize we don't know what juniper looks like. A new house is being erected across the road. The base is mud-clay or brick with castellations into which are lowered pre-carved casements and pinewood doors. Wooden planks form the first floor, tapped into place with alarming speed. In the old days, they prided themselves on assembling entire dzongs without a single nail, just wooden dowels and dovetailing. When a house falls into disrepair and dereliction all the wood rots away or is used for burning, and what remains is the little grey stumpy castle of the foundations. A new building looks old in three years, an old one new with fresh paint. Far below, chillies drying on a roof have been arranged into a message: 'I love Sonam' it says, and around it a huge scarlet heart shape, made of chillies.

The Escher-like quality of the roofs of the dzong, crowding out the sky, magnificently painted and carved – Escher's picture of serfs plodding ever upwards in an Italianate tower, each flight of steps up somehow arriving at the bottom again, has haunted me ever since I first saw it.

Chapter Nine

A Different Place to Stay

We are standing in the middle of a stream: my half-washed socks are dripping on a rock. A bit more beating and slapping and a slow strangling to get the water out and then they'll be fresh as the cowslips in the meadow. We've reached this camp site in daytime, and around us the tents are being erected. Through field-glasses we can make out an imposing building, like a small stately home, about half a mile away against a low wooded hill.

'That's the second King's summer palace,' says Namgay. 'It's closed now.' The windows are shuttered, but it all looks in good condition. It's fenced off, or we would have walked there and snooped around. It's getting more and more difficult to follow the trail exactly.

'Is this Gyacha?'

'No, Gyetsa.'

'Would they have pronounced it differently?' I wonder.

Keeping fairly spruce on the trek. A little shampoo, or just plain mountain water cleans all our clothes. Drying them is a problem as we're always moving on. Part of the fun of camping is working out routines; the fewer possessions the better. By the end of the trip I have given away almost everything: the army boots, my field glasses, thick jerseys and shirts. Only the socks remain.

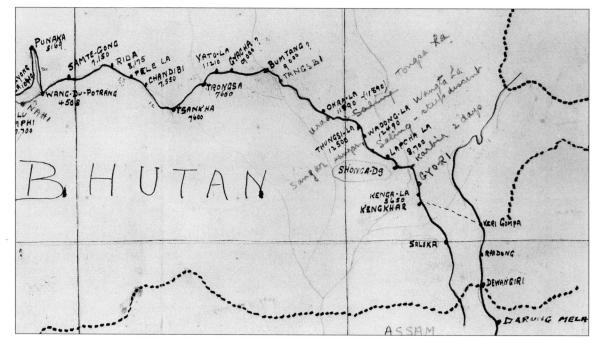

Grandpa's map showing the second half of their journey.

We splosh back to the bank, and from Maybe's rucksack we extract Grandpa's map. Their camp site was below the summer palace... it must be here, as Tongsa was the winter palace. The trouble with following a new road is that we are having to miss out some of their route, although not a murmur of protest did we offer as we drove, rather than walked, over the Yato La Pass at 11,000 ft. (We could have trekked and ridden, I suppose; but we felt strangely compelled to go by Jeep.) Their journey took two months compared with our rushed timetable of three and a half weeks, giving us precious little time to stand and stare. Filming always takes an inordinate chunk out of each day, but we don't mind, as without the film we wouldn't be here at all. The crew work from before dawn to midnight, loading, listing, checking, preparing, carting tripods and sound equipment and generally behaving like heroes. They are all tough trekky chaps, used to filming all over the world, although I've noticed that the last three to go to bed are always our producer Laura, Maybe and me.

At Gyetsa we've all got the chance to rearrange our kit, and re-pack our bags. Everybody has different methods. I would have made only an average filing clerk: but still, to have separate carrier bags for shirts, socks, writing things, cameras, washing things, is the acme of orderliness. In the midnight hours, you must be able to put your hands on something even if it's groped for in the dark: and chaos is the parent of despair.

Maybe and I squeeze into my tiny single tent to talk. When it was very cold at the beginning of the journey, we squashed together under one blue nylon roof, dossing down among our boots and bum-bags to keep warm. We're only six months apart in age and have known each other for so long that we feel like sisters. We went to different boarding schools, but our families always met up in the holidays, when we had all returned from India or the Far East. Our mothers, seven years apart in age, were sent home from India and Sikkim to go to school in England; their holidays were spent in Devon with an elderly couple, but because of the age difference they only overlapped there for a year. The world was starting to change by the time we were born after the Second World War – the Empire was beginning to dismantle itself, and aeroplanes rather than ships began to be used for ferrying personnel to and fro. Suddenly, nowhere was very far away any more. Even I find it hard to think of the five-week journey by troopship to reach Hong

Despite every good intention, we find it very hard to keep our diaries up to date at the end of each day. However it's very important, as I find that nothing matches the immediacy and accuracy of a journal written at the time. Photographs are good aides-memoires, but recorded thoughts are equally vital to accurate recall. Maybe is wearing Joan Mary's own waistcoat made from a Swati blanket, which came here on the first journey. I am in the gho that made the children laugh in Thimphu.

Kong, when now it's only a day away. We were never separated from our parents for very long and consequently we know them far better than Joan Mary and Beatrice knew Thyra and Leslie. But they were terrific letter-writers in those days; their descriptions and drawings compensated for telephone calls (which you couldn't make anyway), and proved far more durable. Then, in the endless moves, our families lost luggage; boxes were stolen or broken, furniture was smashed or dropped on to quaysides or sunk, trunks full of documents went astray. In the end, nothing remains except memories, and when they go you have to start again at the beginning.

The porters have dragged a telegraph pole over to the bonfire. As the evening goes by, we shunt it into the flames little by little, like Bugs Bunny eating a carrot. The heat is phenomenal; we had got used to the little rhododendron branches. My socks steam attractively on twigs near the embers. No matter how late we stay up, one of the porters has to make sure the fire is damped down properly. Before they go to bed they roast themselves front and back before the flames, casting giant flickering shadows into the dewy tents; then, with all the heat in themselves, they wrap up quickly in a blanket to keep as much of it for as long as they can.

When we leave the next morning there's no sign, apart from the ashes of the fire, that anyone has been here at all. Scrupulously clean, deliberately undamaged, not quite only leaving footprints and only taking memories, but not far from it. I take meadow flowers to put in my hat-band; edelweiss and asters, primulas, lichen, even nice-looking leaves. There is a school of thought that you should never pick a flower or a shell or a leaf from anywhere, but you have only to stand in the vastness of those faraway meadows to know that two daisies gone are not going to make a bean's worth of difference to the greater plan.

We owe so much of our British and European gardens to the early plant collectors of the Himalayas. Perhaps in an ideal world (a different world) noone would have the curiosity or enthusiasm to bring flowers and trees and crops back from half-way across the globe. Sometimes it's gone wrong: New Zealand would rather that the humble gorse bush hadn't been introduced from Scotland for hedging, as now it rampages all over their grazing land. Most travellers used to bring back seeds or pods, cuttings, seedlings, anything that would survive long sea journeys, and our world is immeasurably richer for the cross-pollination. Just occasionally, a part of the world remains the way it always was: the Galapagos Islands, Antarctica, maybe tiny atolls and coral islands in some of the seven seas. But people, like ants, busy, organized, ambitious, curious, started travelling and bartering as soon as they knew how and only our varying climates now prevent identical flora and fauna appearing the world over.

Maybe's very good at flowers and we are always stopping to inspect a tiny leaf or peer at distant blossoms. She's keen as well on altitude readings; her grandfather's true granddaughter. In fact, by some oversight we have left the Himalayan flower book in London, which is extremely irritating. I wish it were blue poppy season. Perhaps they sell seeds in England? Grandpa's favourite flower was the cornflower. He used to wear one in his buttonhole. How nice men look with buttonholes! My father's favourite of all time is the gardenia.

Maybe and I have turned into Two Fat Englishwomen, shambling about, talking sporadically, dozing when possible. Namgay is infinitely kind and patient and seems to know the answers to most of our questions.

'What wild animals are there round here Namgay?'

'Musk deer, wild boar, blue sheep. Each village has a leopard or two nearby. They come out at night and sometimes take a dog.'

Poor dog! But how thrilling to be in leopard territory. (Roaring about in a Jeep is not the best way to look out for wild animals, and we never see one.) Large sections of Bhutan are designated as wildlife reserves. The kingdom used to be called the Land of Medicinal Herbs; homeopathic and natural

Because it is only early autumn, the yaks are still grazing in high
pastures and we don't see as many as we'd like. If the camel is the Ship of
the Desert, the yak is the Tank of the Mountains. Their moody unpredictability
is easily handled by their keepers, in this case a charming boy.

remedies are widely used today. The more we find out about Bhutan, the more fascinating it becomes. We had hoped to break into our itinerary to visit Gantey, where the endangered Black-necked cranes arrive every year at exactly the same time to build their nests; apparently they circle the dzong (clockwise of course) three times before they land. But time is always running out, as fine as the sand from a mandala, and we must press on.

Probably because we really have got to know the blue nylon tents inside out, Namgay has arranged for us to lodge in a village house in Ura, which is where we're aiming now. This will be wonderful, having a chance to see inside an ordinary family home and to sleep under a real roof that doesn't belong to an hotel. Our spirits are high as we bomb along the Thimphu–Tashigang Highway: the name rather belies the road, which is only two lanes wide, but none the less remarkable for that. Lovely modern Bhutanese music is playing and the group pictured on the cassette box is as groovy as any band in the UK, only in national costume. The road begins to straighten out from the hairpin bending of the higher mountains, and broad undulating pastures stretch away, dotted with cows and chalets like pictures of Switzerland in the last century. Buses take people to and from towns and markets, but occasionally someone shoots past on a motorbike or Vespa. Any vehicle going anywhere gives lifts to people. A tractor comes towards us driven by what appears to be Genghis Khan, pulling a trailer crammed full of uniformed schoolchildren. In my mind I am always comparing life here with life at home: in almost all contests Bhutan wins hands down. Hardly any traffic, fresh natural food, no television, no advertising hoardings (but we did see a sign misspelling 'household items' as 'itmes', and 'itmes' they've remained). No litter (well, not much), lots of temples in full use, respect for elders, healthy free-range animals, no chemical fertilizers... the list goes on and on, not forgetting, of course, children, who leave school speaking at least three languages fluently and can quote Shakespeare. Perhaps part of the traveller's condition is to fall in love with far away lands and remain in love until the next encounter.

The bus ahead of us is carrying the crew, who sleep like the dead when being moved from A to B. It grinds to a halt and so do we. A dusty road leads the way to the right, down to a valley, wide and bright in the evening sun. We all get out, put on our backpacks and set off towards Ura and the hospitality it offers us.

From half a mile away, Ura looks extraordinarily like a small suburb of Tunbridge Wells: large, well-spaced houses, neatly laid out with tall trees between them, small roads and paths separating them from each other. But in a most un-Tunbridge Wells way the temple looms over them, not huge compared with other dzongs we've seen, but twice as high as the houses and six times as large. The village has kindly agreed to the chaps in nylon tents camping in the forecourt of the temple; there they will pitch the dining tent as well, so our stay in a village house will be more like being at a B & B.

Interested faces stare at us from windows, children climbing on each others' backs to get a better look; but the curiosity is entirely friendly and the staring is not rude, only inquisitive. The light fades as we walk up the earthen paths under willows, past picket fences, over a tiny stream to Mrs Wangmo's house. Dogs and chickens run free in the narrow lanes and alleyways, crows and puppies tussle over scraps and the odd calf walks confidently through us. Mrs Wangmo is waiting at her front door, which is at

Above: Mrs Wangmo, our hostess during our short stay in Ura. She hates having her picture taken, ducking her head shyly out of shot. This is a rare view of her handsome kind face. The shining dark floorboards and dimly lit rooms of her house remind me of a Dutch interior painting, filled with calm and order.

Left: The village of Ura looking like Tunbridge Wells. Mrs Wangmo and her daughter Ugyen live in the house below the trees beneath the temple. The dancing girls who welcomed the Weir expedition, 65 years ago, would have started from where this photograph was taken.

115

first-floor level, approached by steep stone steps, then a nearly vertical wooden staircase made of steps cut into a tree trunk, and shiny as silk from much use. I'm rather nervous about staying with people when all I can say at all accurately is 'Kadinche la,' thank you very much. Mrs Wangmo seems to be about forty-five but it's hard to tell. She is more elegant and grown-up than we are – perhaps it's her formal dress and courteous double-clasped handshake. Her daughter Ugyen is just inside and we bow and clasp hands, all smiling and wishing we had each other's language. The house doesn't really start on this floor; we climb up another steep wooden ladderway before we reach the living quarters. It's nearly dark in here but they have lit a candle on the landing and we've got our torches. There is very little furniture, just plain, wide dark floorboards, shutters at the windows and the sweet smell of a hayloft or oast house. We will be sleeping in the temple room, so we take off our boots and leave them outside on the landing before we go in to the shrine.

An altar takes up most of one side, rich with buddhas, butterlamps, paintings, holy scripts, flowers and rice offerings. The walls of the room are, I think, blue; one is painted with a large depiction of the Green Tara, my mother's favourite Buddhist goddess. There are photographs of the present King, the Dalai Lama and more deities pasted above where our bedrolls will be put. High in the corner are stacked thin eiderdowns, blankets and mats. Ugyen at once pulls them out and starts making up a place for us on the floor and we add our Karimats and sleeping bags; then she brings pillows, and we all stand around beaming at the lovely cosy nest. We mime how we will go to eat supper and return later, and we put on our boots again and climb down the ladders, whose steps are so small that our clumpy boots can hardly get a purchase. It has become very cold again: our breath clouds before us in the torchlight and we step carefully to avoid the sleeping dogs lying all over the road.

Boys and puppies surround the dining tent, shooed away in mock anger by Namgay. Later we see him doling out biscuits to them and they rush off crowing. There is a ring around the full moon tonight, which means rain is on the way. Clasping hot-water bottles under our jackets, we walk back to Mrs Wangmo's. She and Ugyen are waiting up for us and invite us into the kitchen. Again, no furniture; cooking pans stacked neatly in one corner, a huge sort of garlic press the size of a milking stool, a loom with half-woven cloth in it. Ladles in many different sizes hang above the stove, which is on the ground set before a shelf and fuelled like an Aga through a removable hotplate. They brew up some hot milk for us and we all sit on the ground on small rugs and somehow converse with the greatest ease. Ugyen is about twenty-four we guess, and the only daughter of the family. Her two brothers (shown to us in photographs) have left home – one is a lama and one a teacher. Ugyen never received an education and she wrings her hands to show us how wretched she feels at the lack of it and how much she would have loved to study. Two tiny grey kittens advance in crab-like hops and bounds, and chase each other round the stove. The fire hisses and cracks. We say goodnight and 'Kadinche la' for the milk. The lavatory is a long-drop, just a precarious wooden cupboard jutting out from the third floor. When we're in our sleeping bags, Ugyen comes in and puts heavy white eiderdowns over us as well. She lights a candle on the altar and goes out, closing the door.

Above: The elaborate altar which is the centrepiece of the shrine room
where we sleep. Ugyen has laid out the small brass dishes for water: you can
just make out the sculpted butterlamps, peacock feathers and flowers.
The alcoves to left and right are neatly stacked with holy scriptures and there
are several buddhas and manifestations represented in statues and pictures.
It's an enormous privilege to sleep in such a revered place and we remove
our shoes and speak in lowered voices.
Left: Our dear friend Ugyen waving from the landing window.

Chapter Ten

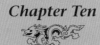

The Kindness of Strangers

Very early, a cock starts to crow outside the window. Rays of sunlight streaming through cracks in the shutters stroke the altar; the golden Buddha gleams: small water dishes, neatly stacked, wait to be set out and filled later by Ugyen. Maybe is still asleep. The cock's crowing is joined by the now-familiar quiet droning of someone spinning prayer wheels and chanting; the sound is coming from several hundred yards away where the temple sits in the misty morning light. Our shrine-room door creaks open and Ugyen comes in with a tray of yak butter tea and cracked wheat. The tea is more like a soup, cream of mushroom soup, slightly salty and thick and delicious. She has made an excellent kind of popcorn, rice or wheat heated till it explodes – puffed wheat, I suppose. This counteracts the saltiness of the tea and is crunchy and quite filling.

My small friends, who materialise out of thin air as soon as I sit down to draw. Like all children everywhere, they have to get closer than close, breathing and squashing and murmuring. At one point a small boy climbs onto my back for a better view of what is now a rather dismal and wobbly drawing of a chorten. I bitterly regret not being able to converse with them. When the school bell rings they rush off in a muddy stampede.

We've got a good day ahead of us exploring Ura and meeting people. In my grandfather's report to the Indian Government (marked 'Secret – Political Department') Ura was 'on the route which had not been previously travelled in its entirety by Europeans'. It is 14½ miles from Bumthang, the site of the investiture, and by the time the expedition crossed the Sheta La Pass and descended into the village, they had travelled nearly 230 miles since their journey began five weeks earlier. At Ura, Grandpa wrote there was '... good camping ground for two regiments. Good water, fuel available from woods a mile away. Wheat, barley, buckwheat and straw available in limited quantities'. As they approached over the icy ground through a thin blizzard, they were met by twelve village girls who had come out to greet them and sing them in for the last 2 miles. 'Ura is a large village of some seventy houses,' wrote Grandpa, and Granny added in her diary, '... very picturesque. Yet another village of bamboo had been built for us. A monastery, not a very imposing one, was tucked away on cliffs some miles distant. Lovely country... a little snow and ice, but in the cold clear frosty air the houses showed themselves to be much better than the ordinary. We noticed paling fences here for the first time...'.

The fences are still everywhere, painted picket fences enclosing flowers and vegetables in neat, garden-sized fields. They are harvesting turnips. The

---

Two children watch us curiously as we set up the camera for some filming around Ura. There is no danger in these quiet villages and tiny children are safe all day, wherever they go. The hills behind are more wooded now than they were when Grandpa wrote his report to the Government of India. Now there are new tree-planting policies, underpinned by the present King's decision to preserve as much of their ancient woodland as possible.

green leafy heads are sliced off, leaving a small disc of turnip attached to the stem and leaves, and then hung or spread out to dry to make winter turnip-top soup, a great delicacy. The tuber is cooked or eaten raw like a giant radish, fairly hot and refreshing when offered in thin slices. Women are doing the turnip cutting. We all grin and wave at each other over the walls and fences. Some of them have tiny babies slung around them, but more often the older children look after the little ones, carting about stout toddlers with infinite care and patience. Because there are no wheeled vehicles here, the paths and streets are often only wide enough for two people to pass. Rough pavements lead through alleys over what are probably drains, but the water flows sweetly and they don't smell.

chorten in Ura by well

You can see the structure of the houses very well at such close quarters. The open-air loft stores a multitude of family possessions but at this time it's given over to drying the turnip tops. Chillies are everywhere, threaded like Christmas decorations on to long strings and hung to dry off balconies, at windows, over doors. A red-painted roof turns out to be merely covered with chillies. There are masses of

Above: Turnips being harvested and prepared for drying.
Eaten raw, they taste like large delicate radishes. The woman wears a
hat which is peculiar to the more eastern regions of Bhutan. The solid
stone construction of houses and barns is very similar to that used
in Yorkshire, Dumfries or the Cotswolds.
Left: My sketch of the chorten at Ura.

flowers, growing out of crevices on walls, blooming in the shadows by weathered iron-studded doors, nodding in quiet courtyards. Creatures amble along, grazing or dozing, but when a fierce looking *dzo*, a cross between a yak and a cow, is led through, the cows take fright and shepherd their calves to safety. Dzo are used for ploughing, their extra strength enabling them to pull the thin ploughshares through sticky clay soil. When I settle down in the shade of a tree to sketch a small chorten by the village well, I am at once surrounded by children, who examine me closely, leaning against my legs and shoulders, climbing over me for a better look at my rather wobbly drawing. Keeping up a stream of comments, they try out some English words: 'Tree!' 'Boy!' 'You!' 'Hallo!', but when a bell rings they charge off back to their classroom. Somewhere above me, unseen young monks are learning the scriptures by rote, chanting aloud in an upstairs room.

Namgay has arranged for us to ride on a yak but it will mean travelling a few miles to Shingkar, a neighbouring hamlet, where someone has been persuaded to bring one down from the summer pastures.

'Will we be able to ride it?'

'Yes, it is quite tame, trained for riding, no problem,' he answers confidently.

I've ridden a yak once before in the Valley of Shimshal in the Karakorams. Fifteen years ago I walked there, with two young English companions and five porters. By the time we arrived, a hellish slog over some very tough terrain, the headman of Shimshal had brought his favourite yak down from the mountains to carry me into the village. He loved his yak dearly, calling her by pet names and leading her all the way. He fed her treats from a cloth he kept wrapped in his coat, and although she groaned and grunted a bit, she walked beautifully with a gait more like a camel than a cow. I very much wanted Maybe to have a go at riding a yak.

The village of Shingkar is surprising. On the top of every house is a solar panel about the size of a music stand, to help heat the water. They look incongruous in such a rural setting, where people are winnowing barley by hand, thumping the grain out on woven mats with wooden sticks linked in the middle like martial arts weapons. There is an Austrian forestry project near here, and we've heard of other schemes assisted by the Dutch and the Danes. A small crowd has gathered at the edge of a field where a furious-looking yak is tethered, jerking about on its string, blankets tied loosely on its back. Namgay gets aboard with some difficulty, the yak behaving very badly and looking crosser by the minute. It lurches about, then sets off across the field in fits and starts. In five minutes he's back, with a look of disgust on his face. 'This yak is too clumsy,' he says, and the idea of us riding it is quietly dropped. I take a handful of grain to feed the animal, who has now become docile and indifferent, half asleep in the hot sun. It refuses my proffered gift by snorting it all over the dusty ground. Unharnessed, it shakes itself like a dog coming out of the water and wanders off to graze.

Back at Ura, women have been shearing sheep in pens beside the village green. They treat the animals gently: if a young one is anxious about the ordeal, they bring it to stand alongside an older ewe to learn the ropes. Two or three women attend each animal, one holding the head in her lap, another keeping its legs still while the sleek black scissors snip away the creamy wool. One of the old women is wearing a distinctive black sheepskin tied to her back. 'I could discover no reason for this,' wrote Granny, who observed that all the singing girls were wearing these woolly black attachments. 'Perhaps it was to protect the back from a load when being carried and became thus a part of their village dress.'

'Namgay, what is the black sheepskin for?'

He talks quietly to the old woman, who hoots with laughter.

'She says she doesn't know.'

The sheared sheep leap to their feet looking as slim as rabbits and join their companions. Weaving, carding and spinning goes on all the time. All the girls know how to make some bit of clothing, although their wardrobes are supplemented by vivid lycra sweaters and knitted hats from India. Most people wear trainers or rubber boots under their robes. Ancient and modern costumes complement each other, and it's only worth commenting on because it is new to our Western eyes. The developed world's dress for men, a suit and shirt, is only complete when a very ancient and useless piece of decoration is added in the shape of a tie. That 4-foot strip of cloth is so important in the West that people are sometimes thrown out of buildings for not wearing one.

I've wrapped up some tiny presents to give our hosts: a satin bag and a bottle of duty-free scent for Mrs Wangmo, and lipstick, mascara, eyeshadow and nail varnish for Ugyen. Into Ugyen's parcel I also slip a little gilt chain from which is suspended a semi-quaver in diamanté; I don't think they notate music as we do in the West, so it will be a rather inscrutable symbol. We sit on our bedrolls on the shrine-room floor and apply the make-up to Ugyen's handsome face, with its high, broad cheekbones and unfurrowed brow. Like all Bhutanese women, her hair is cut short into a fringe and pudding-basin bob. She looks in the hand mirror and laughs. I've noticed that she is already wearing nail varnish which is chipping off. She looks at our clothes, turning them in her hands, examining the seams. The man-made fleece jackets we have are much admired, being light and warm to wear, washable and hardy. She could have had my trainers but they were too small. Outside there is a low babble of voices and when we go downstairs, a small group has assembled carrying things we might like to buy, raided from their houses. It's not permitted to take antiquities out of Bhutan, and some of these things look very old.

'Namgay, will you ask how old this dagger is?'

A murmured consultation follows. 'It's quite new, actually.'

A mother comes chasing her young son who has hauled a family heirloom, a beautifully woven kira, to the impromptu saleroom. She grabs it back, rolls her eyes at us, clips him round the head and takes it away. We will buy only from the actual owner, and only cloth that has been woven recently. The crew are quite beady about spotting attractive 'itmes' and a flurry of money changes hands. The denomination is *ngultrum*, the same value as an Indian rupee, but while the rupee is accepted in Bhutan, the ngultrum is not valid tender in India, reminding me slightly of Scottish banknotes in England, which, if you offer them, are always returned as if you are a bank robber. We hand out more crayons and pens, each received with both hands and stowed away into the robes. We've bought lots of sweets, which are a treat here where sugar doesn't form as much of the diet as it does in the developed world. The local alternative is chewing betel nuts, which eventually wrecks their teeth. A wad is made of a leaf smeared with white lime paste (the same stuff you paint on walls), the lovely veined nut is cut and prepared with an implement which looks like an oyster opener. The betel nut is then

Overleaf: The people of Ura. Even though traditional clothes are supposed to be worn at all times, the odd non-Bhutanese shirt appears like this one on the enchanting small boy in the middle. All our porters wear trousers and sweatshirts while we are trekking, changing formally into their ghos when entering a town. The old woman holds the sheep's head gently and calms it as it is sheared. I love the stylish way she has twisted the cloth round her head.

placed on the leaf and all of it is rolled together and chewed, giving a slight buzz to the consumer. Betel juice is the colour of cochineal, and stains the teeth and lips. I can't bring myself to try any.

Later in the evening, when we are reading and writing diaries before supper, Ugyen draws me aside and puts into my hands an orange woven cummerbund, a *kera*, which she has made herself. She watches me, smiling anxiously, as I try to thank her, admiring it through tear-blurred eyes. She and her mother know we are leaving tomorrow: will we stay for lunch as they are going to prepare a traditional Ura lunch for us? We accept readily; but my heart is already heavy at the thought of leaving.

Packing the next morning is made extra gloomy by rain drumming down, turning the paths into muddy gutters. Ugyen goes out to milk her little cow, after her calf has had her fill. They stand under the dripping barn opposite, the milk swooshing into a plastic bucket, the calf sheltering under her mother's chin, Ugyen on a low stool filling half a pail in five minutes. In Mrs Wangmo's kitchen, the lunch preparations are under way. Buckwheat, mentioned earlier by Grandpa, is ground into flour, then mixed with water into a thick, dryish paste, like fresh pasta. The giant wooden garlic press has been drawn into the cooking area and as the paste is pushed into its bowl-sized drum, the plunger pushes it down through tiny holes and long beige noodles coil out underneath. Mrs Wangmo sits on the cross-bar to force the mixture through as Ugyen prepares the next load. The noodles are par-cooked in boiling water, drained and set aside to keep warm.

An old man, a neighbour, has appeared, having got wind of a good lunch being made, and he settles by the fire offering advice which, from Mrs Wangmo's sharpish rejoinders, we can tell is useless and unwanted. The kitchen is dark, with light coming only from the stove and a high, rain-splashed window. The grey kittens watch from behind saucepans. Eggs and onion-tops are now quickly fried in oil, a little salt added, then beaten eggs and a little more peanut oil. This mixture is added to the buckwheat noodles, turned around and over by hand and served in dishes with chilli sauce. To drink there is sour whey, which is a little like thin yoghurt to taste and very good. They've provided us with forks, but copying their example we eat with our fingers. It is delicious, and we accept second helpings, watched closely by the neighbour who holds out his bowl. Mrs Wangmo taps it away with her spoon; only when we have finished will she and Ugyen eat anything.

Sitting on mats round the stove, we can hear the porters beginning to take our luggage out of the shrine-room across the landing and down the steep wooden stairs. The bus and the Jeep have ground their way on to the village green, churning up mud. The camp has been struck from the temple courtyard, and extra rations of biscuits have been handed out by the cooks. On the veranda by the turnip tops we say goodbye to Mrs Wangmo and Ugyen, all of us holding on to hands for longer than absolutely necessary. Mrs Wangmo mimes her sorrow at us leaving and entreats us to come again. She brings out a white scarf to wave from the veranda till we're out of sight. Ugyen stands forlornly in the rain beside the bus. I take out a white hanky and wave until we can't see her any more. She stands with one arm raised, getting smaller and smaller. The children have run back to their homes but Ugyen is still standing there, waving.

Chapter Eleven

The Destination Reached

As we clomp through the sodden dripping pine forests towards our last night under canvas, the rustling waterproof rainhood seems to catch my thoughts and force them to run round and round my head like a hamster in a wheel. Rain-soaked plumes of larch and spruce whip our cheeks and eyes. My horizons have closed down to the boots of the porter ahead and the sopping wet copper bracken around us. The valleys are shrouded in mist, damp ravens croak from the tops of trees. Germans have a special word for tree top: *wipfel. Gipfel* is the top of a mountain. Wipfel and gipfel. The French have a special word for the back of the neck, *la nuque.* I haven't done enough drawing on this journey. Somehow I'd imagined long afternoons sketching dzongs and porters, maybe even having a go at learning to weave, or trying to make a buddha from clay. Constantly being separated from our luggage

---

We are soaked, even through our nylon anoraks. The pale mauve
poppy-like flowers are called cosmos: I pick some to liven up the dining tent.
The rucksack on my back I pronounce 'rook-sack' as I was taught it as a
German word, from 'ruck' meaning back and 'sack' meaning pack.
Easier to say backpack really. Maybe and I are looking at the tents
which seem to be pitched in a shallow lake.

means that drawing things have often whizzed on ahead, trussed up in the excellent, black heavy-duty plastic kit bags, among jumbled clothes and ungiven presents. By the time we reach the meadow where we're spending the night, the blue dining tent has been put up and all our sad sacks and rucksacks and bedrolls neatly stored inside. Our first job is to identify our luggage, pick a tent and creep in like a dog to start making a nest for the night. Some of the tents have started to leak and the rain-darkened sky makes midnight out of the late afternoon. The under-mattresses are wet. Whisky seems to be the only answer.

On the map we can see that we have leap-frogged Bumthang, the object of our expedition and are now approaching it from the other side. Ura was, for my grandparents, the beginning of the long trip home, after the investiture had taken place. No matter: we wouldn't have missed Ura's kindness for the world and it's fitting that the end of our journey should be at one of the holiest shrines in all Bhutan. The Bumthang valleys are renowned for their beauty. Apple orchards that produce excellent cider; German and Swiss aid programmes have enabled the farmers to capitalize on cheese-making, apricots and honey. *Apfel*, the German word for apple, joins wipfel and gipfel as I spread out my groundmat: my head is like a beehive. It's sometimes very hard to read up on a place you long to visit and to make sense of anything. After a visit, everything is fascinating ('Look, that must have been photographed from above the dzong looking eastwards!'); but before, the words sit like dumplings in the front of the forehead and refuse to be digested.

Outside in the grey deluge, pale mauve poppy-like flowers are waving cheerfully like something from a Fellini film. Around them are wild strawberries and cotoneaster. Over by the cook's tent supper preparations have started. They've managed to get a good fire going and they're all catching up on the Ura gossip as they chop vegetables and mix hissing chilli paste into delicious-looking soup.

'Mindu, what is that squeaking noise?'

Mindu puts down his ladle, and pulls a tiny puppy out from under a sack. It's only a baby, but Mindu bought it and is going to train it to be a good camp follower. He feeds it scraps, and the porters and assistant cooks scratch its ears with strong woodsmen's hands and laugh kindly at its floppy paws.

Through the downpour the kitchen tent is hardly visible from the rest of the camp, and the dunny has been placed far away at the top of a small steep bank which has had thoughtful steps hacked into it. Dashed by boots and raindrops, the steps have turned into a Cresta run of glossy clay. Despite this, we are in good spirits. I pick some mauve poppies for the table, a tilly lamp is lit, we all steam gently round a game of liar dice. The poppy-like flowers are called cosmos, I discover from a pamphlet: the Ura women wear sheepskins on their backs so they can use them as bedding: the name of the village nearest this camp is Membartsho. Everything is accessible, friendly. The peace of the spiritual Bumthang valleys has already begun rocking us to sleep.

It rains solidly for another day. Grey steel stair-rods fall effortlessly down, soaking us through no matter what you hold over your head. Bumthang village appears through the steamed-up windows of the Jeep, closed, grey, shrouded in moisture. The Udee Guest House is very small but can just fit us all in, even the porters and cooks – no pony men now as we have no ponies. The house is made entirely of pine: floors, walls, ceilings. There are small wood-burning stoves in the bedrooms; the communal bathroom has duck-boards on the floor, a bucket and a rather effective shower. The crew call for cheese on toast by the ton, eating as though their necks were cut. We put all our boots and socks to dry around the big stove downstairs, waiting impatiently for the downpour to lighten. We have arrived on the third and last day of the *Tshechu*, the annual religious ceremony which has music and dancing, feasting and festivities. That's why the village street looked grey and closed: everyone is two miles down the valley at the Tshechu.

The rain has stopped but it's nearly dark now. It appears we have missed this extraordinary festival by a day: but Namgay comes with the news that today was too wet for everybody, so the last day is scheduled for tomorrow. Everything works together for good in the end. Just down the road from the guest house, at a crossroads, is a shrine enclosing three huge, groaning prayer wheels, spinning forever, powered by the rushing stream which dashes under them on its journey towards the Bumthang River. The pavilion which houses them has an eternally open door, so you can go in at any time and stand listening to the rolling drums spinning, the bells at their heads ringing, and the water racing off with blessings for all sentient creatures, including visitors and film crews.

Quite a lot of poetry I learned at school centred round a day at the fair. Come away to the fair! Put on your best clothes, close up the shop, leave the

---

The crowds at the Tshechu clamber onto anything to get a better grandstand view of the dancing. Although there is a carnival atmosphere, the re-telling of familiar sacred stories commands absolute concentration. The dances go on for hours: but only yards away are tea stalls selling drinks and snacks to offer a break in the proceedings.

farm and schoolroom, come lasses and lads, if necessary put Granny into the pram with the baby, but come to the fair! The road towards the small temple grounds where the Tshechu is held is teaming with people; most are walking but one or two grand cars bring local dignitaries, and Vespas buzz about like wasps. There seem to be three separate and simultaneous activities: there is religious dancing; there are tea shops and food stalls dotted among handicraft stalls selling their wares; and finally the fairground, where every kind of game found at a village fête in Britain is in progress. There are card sharpers, dart throwers, coconut shies, raffles, bottle stalls and even bingo, attended by a large rapt crowd. The girls are looking wonderful in their loveliest kiras. Many of the young men are wearing school uniform, and look like the dazzling first fifteen or god-like prefects. There are soft drinks for sale, and local cider and *chang*, a very strong rice beer which smells of gym shoes. It's very crowded and has a holiday atmosphere, everyone shoving and laughing.

In the temple forecourt the crowd is so dense that every wall, pole and rooftop is black with people. Music is playing, slow, drum-rapped, with flutes called *jalings*, long-necked trumpets and *damnyen*, the seven-stringed lute with a dragon's head, fantastically painted. The drums are hand-held,

---

One of the beautiful mythical beast-masks worn by the dancers.
All the colours ought to clash, but don't. The costumes are superb: seeing
them swirling in the sunlight makes me regret our rather restrained western
beige, navy and black. The music is very beautiful and easy to pick up and
hum along to. The trumpets and flutes, rather like bagpipes, make your
hair stand on end. You can buy masks like this, but getting them back
to London is a different matter.

about the size of tambourines, beaten with what look like short shepherd's crooks. Eight girls are dancing and singing solemnly in a line, the same small steppy dance we saw on our first night. Behind them, from a temple door, start emerging mythical figures, men in animal masks, wearing skirts of looped silk scarves and ornate shoulder decorations. The animals' faces are the same as the ones we've seen carved over doorways and under the eaves of dzongs: gryphons, blue lions, eagles, spotted leopards, dragons and tigers. They represent the spirits of the underworld: the villagers have come to gaze at them so that they will recognize them when they see them again after their own deaths. There is a trial being acted out. A poor huntsman, a sort of errant Everyman character, has been brought before the Lord of Death, a terrifying figure on a raised throne, flanked by attendants. No matter how he struggles and pleads, he is held down on the ground by the spirits of the underworld, despite the intercession of a holy clown. At the end of the dance, the whole huge crowd forms a long line, filing past the Lord of Death, offering a small prayer. Although the queue is good-natured and smiling, the moment before the dread throne is awesome, as though for a second each one is looking his own death in the face. Then a moment later it's all over and the supplicant, straightening up from the bow and laughing with friends, moves away. But just for a second it was real.

Outside in the throngs between the temple and the fairground a Jeep is nosing towards us. Out leaps the Commissioner of the Bumthang District.

'Her Majesty the Queen Mother has telephoned me. Are you Colonel Weir's granddaughters? Her Majesty has given express permission that you will be allowed to film inside the holy temples at Kurjey Lhakhang. She has sent me with this news.'

This is a phenomenal kindness. The temples are usually strictly closed to visitors and filming inside is unheard of. The third great shrine at Kurjey, built by the Queen Mother, has only recently been consecrated. When the investiture ceremony took place sixty-five years ago, there were only two temples: the smallest, the holy of holies, the *gompa* or shrine built over the indentation in the rock made by the body of Guru Rinpoche, and a larger temple beside it. They are further along the valley, a mile away from the Tshechu. It is now a golden day in late October. We must imagine how it was as the Weir expedition made its way to the spiritual heartland of Bhutan.

'The weather, which had been threatening for some days past, broke, and we arrived at Bumthang on the 8th February during a heavy snowstorm which somewhat marred the arrangements made by His Highness for our entry. At the top of the Kyi Kyi La [a pass at 11,600 ft] Dasho Nacku, aged about twelve, the younger brother of His Highness, was waiting for us with a log fire and hot tea which was very acceptable in the storm.

'The King met us at the gate of our camp, which we entered over a red silk carpet. Flowering plants, procured from the lower valleys, and trees planted in the ground and hung with oranges struck an incongruous note amid the snow. His Highness stayed for lunch, then he and all his entourage came to dinner that night. Fourteen people was rather a handful for Thyra to cater for at very short notice.

'They had most of their meals (not breakfasts) with us during our stay at Bumthang. Even when they gave a meal, they borrowed our cook and glass and crockery and did everything at our quarters, so there was not much difference.'

So wrote Grandpa to his mother in Scotland. Friday, 13 February was found to be an auspicious day for the ceremony: the programme for the presentation was worked out in consultation with the King and Raja Topgay Dorji, his Deb Zimpön, at what we would call today a working lunch. The day dawned dry and bright: Granny's diary takes up the tale.

'Snow lay thinly on the road in places, but the sky was electric blue and the whole population of Bumthang and the adjacent villages appeared to be making their way in a long line up the valley. Everywhere was excitement. We were mounted on H.H.'s richly caparisoned mules – each saddle-cloth a dream of highly coloured appliqué. The twenty soldiers of the warrior body-guard were in full panoply – gorgeous silk doublets with a black rhinoceros shield hung behind: two swords, and a round iron helmet covered with silk and a multi-coloured silk rope around the base. Immediately in front of us two male dancers sprang lightly, and sang occasionally, not always in time with the two flutes that were being played. A drum was beaten and deep-toned cymbals, like a lovely bell, were clanged at intervals.'

Maybe and I are standing on the huge flat field in front of the three sacred temples of Kurjey. To our right, a long line of hundreds of prayer flags flutter in the sunshine. Behind them is a familiar line of hills – these are the ones we've seen in the big ceremonial photograph they had taken after the event, the same prayer flags in the same position. This is the way they would have approached. We walk slowly forwards.

'Prayer flags by the hundred waved in the breeze and tents had been erected where we were to change from our riding kit. Leslie put on his uniform and cocked hat and we did the best we could to adorn ourselves in our meagre coats and skirts and fur coats. It was already bitterly cold.'

Around the three temples a new wall has been built, with 108 chortens placed at regular intervals along the top, symbols that commemorate Buddha's victory over evil. We enter the courtyard through a whitewashed gateway. It's very hot and still, we can hear crickets chirruping and the grass is quite dry and brown. A handsome cock is pecking and scratching by a bed of zinnias; two small temple boys are washing and refilling vases of marigolds by a pump. They turn and smile, never stopping in their work; they have close-cropped hair and are wearing trainers. Most families send one boy to study and train at the monastery – these two don't look homesick or particularly pious – just two lovely boys, part of the cycle of life and tradition in the only country in the world to uphold a form of Mahayana Buddhism, which used to be called Lamaist Buddhism, as a state religion. Behind the pump a steep flight of steps leads up between the two oldest temples.

'Are these the steps, do you think?' says Maybe. 'They're the only ones here.' Joan Mary, her mother, had told her about the perilous ascent which Granny described in her diary.

'Wonderful decorations had been arranged, with branches of trees and prayer flags stuck into the ground on each side of the main walk to the gompa. The customary red cloth was held in its place by enormous stones over which we occasionally tripped were we not very careful. It was difficult to negotiate the cloth once we reached the flight of steps. It ballooned out, caught by the wind, and it was a dangerous game endeavouring to stamp it back on to any one step. And, of course, several people trying at the same time to follow one another up the cloth invariably came to grief by striking a taut piece suddenly.' Granny and Joan Mary, much given to sudden fits of laughter, must have struggled hard to keep dignified expressions on their faces.

Maybe and I pass the two boys and walk under a shadowy tree and up the steps. We are, in fact, not allowed to film in the holiest shrine, and Namgay has been in hot dispute with a senior monk about us being allowed to enter at all. 'It doesn't matter, Namgay, we can go into the other two temples...', but somehow he wangles it and the monk beams and beckons. Removing our shoes and hats, we enter as the seventeen-year-old Joan Mary continues the story.

'We passed through a dimly lit room that was filled with lamas who peered at us curiously. The ceremony was held in the very holy temple itself, a lovely place with a huge model of Guru Rinpoche on the altar and lots of gold idols and butterlamps all round. Opposite the altar on two brocade-draped thrones sat the King – in wonderful robes – and Daddy. We and the Queen and the other royal ladies sat on one side of the room, and opposite us, in front of a row of Bhutanese officials, sat seven holy lamas dressed in red brocade robes and hats.

'First, ceremonial tea and rice was offered. The tea-carriers, to ensure against poisoning, tested their brew by pouring a little from each massive

---

Duties in the monasteries are regularly delegated to quite young boys. Every day the altars are re-dressed, offerings are made anew, lamps refilled and the blazing marigolds have their water changed and stems scrubbed to revive them. Maybe and I are sitting in the dark shade of a tree to escape the heat of the October sun. The sounds of the boys chattering, brass vases clanking and water splashing is refreshing: our minds are travelling in time to years ago, trying to reconstruct the scene as the Weirs walked past this very spot, carefully negotiating the billowing red carpet.

silver teapot into their left hand and tasting it. Tea was poured for the King and then for everyone according to rank. The monks sang a long impressive grace in a low, moaning chant – it was very beautiful.

'Then Daddy read his speech, in Urdu, which was translated into Tibetan by his personal assistant Norbu, and pinned on the KCIE. The King made a short speech in Hindi, thanking the government of India and Daddy. Then the present-giving began...'.

Grandpa's formal presents had already been placed in the middle of the floor, and now the officials and subjects added their own 'and the entire floor was quickly covered with bales of cloth and silk, some bags of gold dust, bundles of Tibetan tea, skins, etc...'. Each offering was accompanied by a ritual of ceremonial obeisance and the presentations lasted nearly an hour.

'The ceremony now over,' wrote Grandpa, 'His Highness conducted us down the steps to the tents where luncheon had been arranged. After luncheon, sports, tug of war and masked dances were appreciated by a crowd of 4000 of His Highness's subjects who had collected for the occasion and for the feast that had been prepared for them. A cold ride home was followed by a dinner party I gave to His Highness and family in honour of the occasion.'

Motes of dust hang in the sunbeams thronging the shrine room. We can just make out the holy dint in the rock, and imagine where the thrones were and where the gifts were heaped. I can almost see the rows of chairs, monks, royal ladies and officials and in their midst Granny, Joan Mary and Dagmar in their hats and gloves, gorgeous cloths tumbled on the floor, the chanting lamas, and backlit on their brocade cushions the King and Grandpa, thin wintry light streaming in from the window. There is a low buzz of voices, the sound of the crowd outside waiting patiently in the bitter cold, a murmur

Above:The official group photograph taken after the presentation ceremony.
The King is flanked by Granny and Grandpa, on whose right is the Queen.
Joan Mary in cream with a wide-brimmed hat stands behind them, and
Dagmar is behind Granny. At her left sits Lt. Revel Sinclair. Between Dagmar
and Joan Mary stands Grandpa's personal assistant, Norbu Dhondup.
Completing the front row are the King's half-sisters Ashi Pedon and Ashi
Wangmo; on the extreme left is young Dasho Nacku. His elder brother,
Dasho Dorji, took this photograph with Grandpa's camera.
Overleaf: When it was time to leave Bumthang, the King travelled with
them to the next village to say a final farewell. The last exchange of silk
scarves took place on a wild hillside.

and laughter from the two throned figures. Time is standing still: the booming I can hear is my heartbeat. The senior monk is standing and watching us, waiting politely for us to leave. The temple room glows with a sudden shaft of brilliant sunshine. We bow to the altar and go.

Outside it has become hotter still and we drink from the pump. The temple boys have gone. Two huge chortens concealing the mortal remains of the first two kings of Bhutan stand 50 yards apart in the courtyard. Someone is cleaning out the low wooden guest lodgings for pilgrims at one side of the enclosure. Over a woven bamboo fence the shrine to the third king, the present King's father, stands surrounded by blazing coloured prayer flags, all the colours, all new and bright, red, yellow, green, blue and white. Inside the second and third temples are so many golden deities, painted manifestations, gods and goddesses, saints and mystic consorts, that the great empty shrines seem to be humming with ghostly benevolent presences. The newest and largest temple already feels as though it has stood here for centuries, as old as the first Lhakhang, reputedly built in the eighth century. The walls are not whitewashed, but in every other respect the three temples match and complement each other. Where this huge building stands now sat the waiting crowds, feasting on the grand banquet which was brought round to them, rather like the feeding of the five thousand. Here, on February's snow-flecked ground, rather than today's hot October grass, wrestled the young men we'd seen on the archive film, grabbing each other's arms in their attempts to haul opponents on to the ground. Here they took all the formal ceremonial photo-graphs, as well as friendlier snapshots; and congratulations were offered to the King and Queen, and compliments paid to the two-year-old Crown Prince, who was carried about in great style on a retainer's shoulders. How many times I've thought of this scene, trying to imagine what it was really like... and now we're here and the last pieces of the jigsaw click satisfactorily into place. We sit for a while outside on the sunny steps to the new temple, thinking our thoughts as the sun begins to dip down in the sky. Then we put our shoes back on and set off home, past the long line of prayer flags, for-ever blowing in the light wind.

Chapter Twelve

Leaving for the First Time

The journey back is westwards all the way and as the sun sinks, I make Tapa, our driver, put on my green sunglasses against the distractingly low sunbeams coming in through the windscreen. Our heads twist on our necks as we crane to catch the fleeting views. We crawl up and fly down the highest passes, Yato La, Pele La, Bela La and down into the familiar golden valley of Paro. All the rice and barley has been harvested, and the brown earth shows; winter is not far away now.

We have been invited to lunch by the Queen Mother in her beautiful summer palace below Paro Dzong, not far from the broad, shallow river. Tapa knows the protocol: only the Royal Family may use the long drive under the avenue of trees; other cars turn sharply just inside the gate and bump along over the grass. Dasho 'Benjy' Dorji is there, and the Venerable Mynyak Tulku Rinpoche who blessed our journey, and his sister-in-law. We greet each other with delight – in such a short time we have all become friends.

Ashi Kendum tells Maybe and me about the Queen Mother's palace as we approach through the gardens for lunch. The roses and zinnias are dazzling, but pale in comparison with the gloriously decorated interior of the palace.

The palace is said to be modelled on Padmasambhava's heavenly dwelling-place. It stands in a courtyard with the four small guest houses in the corners and trees in pots. Flower-beds spilling with blooms lie under the walls, and as we walk clockwise round to the entrance, we almost fall over ourselves for staring at its beauty. The Paro Penlop, who welcomed Granny and Grandpa, designed it in the 1920s as a palace for himself and later, for a time, it was used as a royal guest house; now it has reverted to the sole use of the royal family. Its tall pagoda shape reaches gracefully upwards under successive roofs. Inside the colours are intoxicating, every space painted and gilded, any sense of excess offset by the formal arrangements of the rooms. We are joined the Master of Protocol in a grey gho. There is a flurry of activity outside in the courtyard. The Queen Mother has arrived, back from praying in the temple, with the two young princesses and her sister Ashi Tashi.

After softly spoken greetings, the kindest words said, we move to the dining-room, glorious dark orange overpainted with gold. A table spread out at the far end offers salads, orchids, river weed, dumplings, red and white rice, chicken, yak, and European steak and kidney pie and cold meats for those who would prefer it. The Queen Mother has put Maybe and me on either side of her; we talk and talk as though catching up for all the years we and our forebears have missed. The conversation ranges over all sorts of unconnected subjects: the painting of temple statues, the possibility of the King reintroducing a nearly extinct pony to Bhutan, visits to America, and our families. She speaks flawless English: when servants address her, they hold their sleeves over their mouths so their breath won't share the air she breathes.

'Your grandfather was a true friend to Bhutan,' she says softly. 'My father-in-law loved him.' Into my mind flicks Grandpa's report of 1931.

Officials of the Political Committee had written their own comments and notes on attached pages, concerning the 'anomalous position' of Bhutan in relation to the Government of India, and whether Bhutan should be invited to join an Indian Federation. Grandpa had reported how strongly the King opposed closer union with India, and emphasized his own view that it should remain in '... its present indeterminate independent position'. He added that it would not be an auspicious time to attempt to link Bhutan with India; that if Bhutan were not to disintegrate, she must have increased financial support. 'With Chinese pressure on Tibet looming larger on the political horizon, it is necessary to stress the danger to the Northeast Frontier of India if Bhutan collapses.' So, all those years ago Grandpa helped Bhutan to retain her independence, and he is remembered with love and gratitude for that.

We are drinking a superb 1972 claret of the Queen Mother's own label: lemon mousse and meringues are served; branches of the blue berries that Granny loved decorate the table and the sideboards. How can we be so lucky? There are times in life when you pinch yourself and say remember this always, for whatever happens from now on, these moments cannot be taken away: and later on the inward eye can recreate the palace dining-room, Mrs Wangmo's temple room, the distant snows of Chomolhari, the ponies grazing beside the mountain lakes. The Venerable Mynyak Tulku has invited us up to the watch-tower above the dzong to see the museum; the Queen Mother has suggested some more shrines for us to visit, Paro village beckons with its shops crammed full of carvings and weavings. But our time is nearly up in Bhutan.

Back at the hotel the crew have started packing up. Rooms are in semi-organized chaos as each case is crammed with twice the amount it contained before, things having a tendency to multiply and expand when you're not looking. We've got one more bit of filming to do. Near Paro is the most spectacular monastery called Taktsang, the Tiger's Nest, so called because Padmasambhava flew from Tibet on the back of a tigress and landed on a 3000-foot cliff face, bringing Buddhism to Bhutan. The monastery is a shrine for pilgrims and a magnet to all visitors. You can walk up to it, or ride. The film cameras prefer the sight of a nice ambling pony to that of a puffing tourist, so I ride. Namgay and Maybe have decided to have one last shot at fishing – the rivers round here are full of trout, although fishing is rather frowned on by Buddhists.

'What about riding, Namgay?'

'A good Buddhist doesn't ride unless he has to. It's different in the hills. We have a saying: "You're not a proper horse if you don't take your master up. You're not a proper man if you don't walk your horse down".'

The path to Taktsang is wide and sandy, trodden smooth by thousands of feet. Women have spread out mats at intervals along the way, offering tiny things for sale, home-made paintings, ancient locks from their doors, a few old coins, a bit of chain, a ladle. The path rises steeply in lazy zigzags, corners cut by eager walkers who appear to be able to stride up vertical surfaces. My pony is in a trance of indifference, having done this hike so many times before that his long-lashed eyes are sometimes closed. I don't need reins as he plods up, taking rests when he needs them and falling into a deep slumber while the crew organize up-and-past shots, which are just what their name

---

The closed monastery at Taktsang, the Tiger's Nest. How on earth it was built is a mystery. Visitors may walk round the back on hair-raising rocky paths but its doors are closed to most foreigners. High above on the cliff flutter prayer flags dispensing their blessings on us all.

suggests: approaching the camera, then riding past it as it swings round to follow you, so it can see you coming and going. None of the ponies has been taught to back, so when we do the shot again, the pony has to be turned, sometimes on a space the size of a stamp and led back a few yards and turned again. He always looked offended and mutinous: his job is to keep going forward. Hot sunlight dapples down on us: a young family from Derbyshire go past at a cracking pace, unfazed by the height or heat. There is no more tranquil occupation than sitting on a slow pony on a mountain path.

Eventually, hours later, we reach a small, beautiful pagoda with open sides sheltering a huge, apricot-coloured prayer wheel. In the distance, about half a mile away as the raven flies, gripping to the sheer grey rock-face is the extra-

Above: My pony waits outside the little pagoda.
Right: As the silk flags flutter from the spinning prayer wheel, my family's two journeys seem to blend into one, fusing the past with the present.

ordinary Tiger's Nest, three buildings, each positioned more perilously than the next above an unthinkably deep ravine. I get off my beast and gaze across. You can walk all the way round the cliff to Taktsang but you can't go in as it is off limits to most outsiders; and in any case, our filming has taken longer than expected, and we still have the homeward journey to make, down, down to the valley and the evening shadows. There is a crimson prayer flag fluttering high above the pagoda's wooden roof. Inside, like looking out from a saint's pavilion, you can see to the four quarters of the earth. I can see the distant monastery and far-away valleys: the sun is warm on my shoulders. Reaching forward, I spin the great drum and the bell rings with each revolution: spinning and ringing under the red shadow of the prayer flag, spinning and turning, it sends its blessings out ceaselessly on the past, the present and the future.

When we get back to the hotel, it is dusk. Unexpected presents have arrived. From the King, a silk thangka, an album of Bhutanese stamps and a beautifully woven kira, all wrapped in hand-made paper and tied with red and gold ribbons. And from Namgay, that which I had yearned for on the journey: a small, smooth-worn wooden pack saddle for a pony.

Notes

Page 31: Young Lochinvar, the hero of Sir Walter Scott's poem was a tremendously dashing fellow.

'...''we are gone, over bank, bush and scaur;
They'll have fleet steeds that follow'' quoth young Lochinvar.'
Our placid steeds, however, were far from fleet.

Page 43: The lovely hymn 'The day thou gavest, Lord, is ended' has the lines
'The voice of prayer is never silent,
Nor dies the strain of praise away'
in it. The most familiar tune was written by C.C. Scholefield, and the words are by J. Ellerton. I first remember singing it in Malaya when I was six years old.

Page 65: 'The wedding march' from *Lohengrin* by Wagner is justly world famous. 'O mio babbino caro' is from the short opera *Gianni Schicchi* by Puccini. 'Babbino' is a pet name meaning literally little daddy. 'Babbo' is Florentine Italian, and the aria is a heart-wrenching plea from a young woman to her father.

Whenever I travel I take one or two volumes of Anthony Powell's masterpiece *A Dance to the Music of Time*. *The Valley of Bones* deals with the war years and is unexpectedly funny and brilliantly observed. I had the great good fortune to meet another of my heroes Patrick Leigh Fermor at the unveiling of Sir John Betjeman's plaque in Poets' Corner, Westminster Abbey. Between these two great men is to be found the best prose ever written in the English language. Sir John is on a separate and equal pedestal as a poet.

Page 68: 'Continuous as the stars that shine' was Wordsworth's reference to daffodils in his poem of that name. I learnt it by heart when I was very young.